Persons, Rights, and Corporations

Patricia H. Werhane
Loyola University of Chicago

Prentice-Hall, Inc. *Englewood Cliffs, N.J.* 07632

Library of Congress Cataloging in Publication Data

WERHANE, PATRICIA HOGUE (DATE)
    Persons, rights, and corporations.

    Includes bibliographical references and index.
    1. Employee rights.   2. Business ethics.   I. Title.
HD6971.8.W47 1985   174'.4   84–23731
ISBN 0–13–660341–6

Editorial/production supervision and
    interior design by Eva Jaunzems
Cover design by Joe Curcio
Manufacturing buyer: Harry P. Baisley

Printed in the United States of America
10 9 8 7 6 5 4 3 2 1

ISBN   0-13-660341-6   01

Prentice-Hall International, Inc., *London*
Prentice-Hall of Australia Pty. Limited, *Sydney*
Editora Prentice-Hall do Brasil, Ltda., *Rio de Janeiro*
Prentice-Hall Canada Inc., *Toronto*
Prentice-Hall Hispanoamericana, S.A., *Mexico*
Prentice-Hall of India Private Limited, *New Delhi*
Prentice-Hall of Japan, Inc., *Tokyo*
Prentice-Hall of Southeast Asia Pte. Ltd., *Singapore*
Whitehall Books Limited, *Wellington, New Zealand*

For Hillary, Kelly, Pieke, and Stephanie

ACKNOWLEDGMENTS

Excerpts from Chapter One originally appeared in another version in "Formal Organizations, Economic Freedom, and Moral Agency," *Journal of Value Inquiry,* 14 (1980). Reprinted by permission of the journal and its editor.

Parts of Chapter Two originally appeared in another version in "Corporations, Collective Action, and Institutional Moral Agency" in Michael Hoffman, ed., *Corporate Governance: Institutionalizing Ethics* (Lexington, Mass.: D. C. Heath & Co., 1984). Reprinted by permission of the publisher and editor.

Some of the arguments in Chapters Four and Six were originally presented in "A Theory of Employee Rights" in Thomas Donaldson and Patricia H. Werhane, eds., *Ethical Issues in Business* (Englewood Cliffs, N.J.: Prentice-Hall, 1983). Reprinted by permission of the publisher.

Parts of Chapter Five originally appeared in "Accountability and Employee Rights," *International Journal of Applied Philosophy,* 1 (1983). Reprinted by permission of the journal and its editor.

Contents

2

Corporations and Institutional Moral Agency   49

3

Rights, Responsibilities, and Corporate
Accountability   60

PART 2:   THE MORAL STATUS OF
EMPLOYEES

4

Employment at Will and The Question of
Employee Rights   81

5

Employee Accountability and The Limits of Role Responsibility   94

6

Political Rights in Employment: Due Process, Freedom, and Privacy   108

7

Economic Rights in The Workplace: Safety, Fair Pay, Participation, and Meaningful Work   127

8

Implied Contracts in Employment: The Prima Facie Right Not to Be Fired   143

Conclusion: Institutionalizing Moral Agency in Corporations   153

Preface

This book grew out of a long-time interest in three topics: the nature of moral rights, the ontological character of corporations, and the status of employee rights. A study of moral rights and their application to employees in the workplace, an examination of the ontological status of corporations and the so-called rights of such organizations, and an evaluation of the moral relationships between corporations and their employees appear to be fruitful areas of research for many of the ethical issues in business. It is hoped that this book will be a useful contribution to these topics.

The research and writing of this book have been supported by the Philosophy Department and by grants from the Department of Research Services at Loyola University. A number of people have read parts or all of the manuscript and offered invaluable suggestions. I particularly single out Robert Cooke, Thomas Donaldson, Tom Regan, Thomas Wren, and an anonymous reviewer at Prentice-Hall who scrupulously read and commented on a draft of the work. A. R. Gini, Kenneth Goodpaster, Thomas McMahon, C.S.V., David Ozar, and many others have also contributed to the project, albeit in different ways. The manuscript itself, however, its arguments, and the conclusions it reaches are entirely my responsibility.

I would also like to thank especially Catherine Pearson, who helped with the word processor, two patient secretaries, Ruby Murchison and Cynthia Rudolph, without whom there would be no book, and of course the editors of Prentice-Hall, Doris Michaels and Raymond O'Connell, who have provided continued encouragement and support.

P.H.W.

Introduction

This book presents an analysis of the modern business corporation and its ethical relationships with its employees. That the book focuses almost exclusively on this topic is due to the author's conviction that a clear-cut concept of the corporation, a defense of employee rights, and an analysis of the interrelationships between corporations and employees are essential in order to carry on a dialogue in business and in business ethics. The importance of this project cannot be exaggerated. Our economic system depends on the efficient functioning of productive organizations. The vast majority of these are corporations. The products corporations manufacture, the services they provide, the resources and the environment they use make a positive or a negative difference to persons and to society. Economists, philosophers, and political theorists have become increasingly interested in the proper analysis of contemporary corporations. This is the subject of Part One.

Second, corporations are created by, operate because of, and are run by persons—employees, employers, and, to a lesser extent, stockholders. In this country employees have traditionally enjoyed few rights at work. Standardly recognized political rights to due process, to freedom, and to privacy are not universally honored there. Few employees have rights to their jobs, and most can be fired at the discretion of their employer. Worker safety is a continuing problem, and even in the 1980s not all public employees have the right to strike. What the role of an employee is, from a moral point of view, and how respect and human dignity can be instituted in the workplace are the subjects of Part Two.

The study of corporations and their employees raises a most difficult question. Can respect for human dignity be realized in the workplace without sacrificing economic efficiency and innovation? Can one modify employee-employer relationships in such a way as to preserve private ownership, business freedoms, and the benefits of capitalism while clearing up injustices in the workplace?

Traditionally this sort of question has been approached by studying the economic system, that is, capitalism, as a whole. Solutions have classically been what one might term macro–solutions. Some defenders of private enterprise, those commonly labeled "conservatives," argue that the least regulated, freest sort of economy is the most desirable. In this view, if the rights to freedom and to private ownership are to be respected and preserved, rights clearly espoused since the founding of our country, business must be allowed to enjoy these rights by operating in as unregulated a manner as possible. Further, the economic benefits of private enterprise fostered by open competition and economic incentives provide jobs, goods and services, and a high standard of living. These flourish only in a private free-enterprise ("laissez-faire") economy. Interference in business affairs, such as the institution of programs for employee rights, will do irreparable damage to productivity and eventually to the economy as a whole.

On the other side, critics of this view contend that unregulated capitalism perpetuates a number of injustices. One of these about which we will be concerned in this book is the moral treatment or mistreatment of employees. The most radical of these thinkers call for some revision or radical change of the system. This is because they find that all forms of capitalism are inherently unjust or foster injustices so that fairness in the workplace—or indeed anywhere—is not possible within a capitalist economic system.

I shall argue in this book that one need not radically revise our present economic system in order to achieve changes that are both feasible and desirable. Rather, some modifications within our present free-enterprise system, modifications of the organization of corporations coupled with the recognition and voluntary institution of employee rights, will achieve results palatable both to defenders of free enterprise and advocates of workers' rights. A proper analysis of the corporation, of employees in the corporation, and of the relationships between these individuals and the corporation can yield a form of modified capitalism that does justice to employees, that is not inefficient, and that preserves the voluntarism so desirable to defenders of free enterprise.

This book, then, like most books, has some obvious biases. I am biased toward a form of private enterprise because of its economic advantages, its flexibility, and its innovativeness. I am also biased against a purely free market that does not respect the equal rights of individuals, in particular the rights of employees in the workplace. However, I shall not explicitly argue for or defend a version of a modified free-enterprise system, because the subject matter of the book is not an analysis of economic systems *per se,* but rather an analysis of two important components of our economic system, corporations and employees.

The bias in favor of a modified free-enterprise system carries with it another assumption, the assumption that private ownership is not antithetical to achieving a just economic system. Our economic system is based, at least in part, on the principle that persons and organizations have rights to own, manage, buy, and sell properties. "Property" here includes everything from capital to land, goods, and services. Now there are many problems with the notion of private property, some of which I shall discuss briefly in a later section of the Introduction. However, I shall bracket many of these problems in order to make the less grandiose but still important argument that, *given* a private free-enterprise system where a form of private ownership is the prevailing model of property control, a proper organization of corporations and a recognition and exercise of employee rights will yield positive results for the economy and for human rights.

I shall approach this subject through the concept of a moral right. I shall assume that all human beings, and in particular rational adults, have inherent value. Because human beings have inherent value they have certain rights. These rights are moral rights because they are rights that everyone possesses, but they are rights that are not recognized or exercised everywhere. I shall propose that one can make sense out of employee and organizational claims by approaching them through an evaluation of moral rights. Such a defense should not be antithetical to most forms of capitalism, which historically has aligned itself with human rights. Yet this position entails recognition of *equal* employee and employer claims, and this is sometimes less agreeable to defenders of free enterprise.

Why are rights important, even crucial, in the context of business? Businesses function in part because of the work of employees. Without workers to produce goods and to manage things there would be no business. While workers in our society are certainly not mistreated, traditionally *rights* of employees, although constitutionally guaranteed, have not been universally honored in business. Employees cannot always exercise free expression, and they are often denied rights to fair hearings or to other just procedures in the workplace. The reasons that constitutionally guaranteed legal rights are not always extended to the workplace are complex, as we shall see in Part Two. And whether or not one wishes to extend such legal rights in the workplace is a controversy we shall consider in later chapters. But the absence of legal rights in the workplace is paralleled with the absence of recognition that these rights are moral rights and as such should be honored with or without legal mandate. Therefore a theory of employee moral rights is essential to eliminate unfairness in employment practices and to justify employee exercise of moral rights at work.

Moral rights are important in another aspect of business. Persons create the business world. They start businesses, and they form corporations to produce goods and services. Because businesses are developed by and operate on account of persons, businesses, especially modern corporations, sometimes think they have rights, in particular the right to conduct business freely and independently. Moreover, businesses operate in human communities. Because business activities affect persons, businesses have certain societal moral obligations, obligations to persons. As we shall see in Part One, a theory of organizational rights would be invaluable in evaluating the rights and moral obligations of business.

An evaluation of employee and organizational concerns in terms of a theory of moral rights is only one of many approaches, and by no means the *only* legitimate approach, to these issues. Throughout the essay this sort of analysis will be compared with a more utilitarian approach, and some strong utilitarian justifications will in fact be used to bolster certain of the arguments. However, I shall contend that an analysis of employees and corporations through the notion of moral rights is essential to an understanding of the injustices in our present economic arrangement and offers some positive suggestions for the future of a fair economic system.

It will be concluded that any society that recognizes the exercise of equal rights need not inhibit fair treatment and positive human development, even in a private enterprise economy where there is a prevalence of strong productive organizations. One can honor employee and organizational demands equally and respectfully without destroying a capitalist economic system. Freedom and positive human development can be realized for everyone in a society dominated by privately owned economic institutions. But this is possible only if corporate moral development takes place, and only if individual moral rights are recognized and honored on all levels of economic activity. Finally, because this text is primarily addressed to undergraduates and graduate students in ethics and economics, some of the arguments may seem too simple to professional philosophers. However, it is hoped that the book will be useful in focusing attention on two essential components of our economic system: corporations and employees.

A THEORY OF MORAL RIGHTS

In a recent book, *The Mountain People,* Colin Turnbull describes an African tribe, the Ik, in which any notion of human rights seems to have disappeared, if indeed the idea ever existed. The Ik, according to Turnbull, have been isolated in recent years in a mountainous region in Northern

Uganda where survival is difficult at best. Whether or not their isolation and meager surroundings have affected their world view is unclear. In any case, according to Turnbull, the Ik recognize no claims of other human beings. In fact, they do not even acknowledge their own rights, but selfishly take whatever they can in order to survive. Without being a violent society the Ik share nothing. At age three children are no longer allowed to stay or to sleep at home, and are sent out to survive on their own. Mothers steal food from their children and "it is common . . . to see the very young prying open the mouths of the very old and pulling out food they had been chewing."[1] Turnbull tells how one family rejected the attempted return home of a retarded child who was mistreated by her peers because of her disabilities. When she persisted in her attempts, the parents accepted the child and then shut her in the house, leaving her to starve. The treatment of the aged in this society is equally cruel. Turnbull relates how the old are left to die in ravines from which they are too weak to escape. And one of the few sources of entertainment for the Ik is to observe helplessness or infirmity. Seeing an old woman in this condition Turnbull attempted to help her. To the consternation of the other Ik he offered her food and medical care. But the old woman merely laughed at Turnbull and refused assistance. After she died her husband came and stripped her of her last remaining possessions. The old woman accepted without question the convention that she and those who cannot help themselves must die. She had no notion that as a human being she was being mistreated and that she had certain entitlements despite the wretchedness of her situation.[2]

One hopes the Ik are an exception to the human condition, for Icien society illustrates a community in which not only self-respect, human dignity, and the respect for others are missing, but also one in which the *criteria* for evaluating those qualities to which one might appeal in making interpersonal judgments are absent. That is, the Ik lack any notion that human beings including themselves possess certain rights just because they are human, and that they are entitled to exercise these rights and to receive the respect accorded to rights-holders. Without a concept of a moral right the Ik are unable to evaluate their own actions or the actions of others. Thus, the understanding of moral rights is crucial if one is to avoid interpersonal relationships such as those exhibited by the Ik.

Moral rights are important in another respect. If one is to criticize what appears to be inhumane treatment of persons, as in the case of the Ik, or if one is to make moral claims about the way a society or particular

---

[1]Colin M. Turnbull, *The Mountain People* (New York: Simon and Schuster, 1972), p. 261. Copyright © 1972 by Colin M. Turnbull. Excerpts reprinted by permission of Simon & Schuster, Inc.

[2]Ibid. pp. 226–28. At the end of the book (p. 285) Turnbull states, "The Ik are reduced in numbers to only a few thousand . . . so I am hopeful that their isolation will remain as complete as in the past, until they die out completely. I am only sorry that so many individuals will have to die, slowly and painfully, until the end comes to them all."

persons *should* act, one must be able to define the universal entitlements that human beings possess or are entitled to exercise. A moral right is such a concept. To establish that there *are* moral rights is important to evaluate societal injustices and to establish criteria for the fair treatment for all persons everywhere.

MORAL RIGHTS

What is a moral right? Let us begin by defining *basic* moral rights, that is, those rights that are the foundation for any rights whatsoever. Other legitimate moral rights will turn out to be rights derived from basic moral rights. Let us begin by elaborating on an assumption to which we alluded earlier: the assumption that all human beings have value just because they are human. That this is at least intuitively true is easiest to see if we restrict our argument to rational adults. Rational adults have value, one can argue, because they are capable of interests, and because they can make self-conscious choices based on thoughtful decisions. Rational adults can analyze their own actions, they can control and change their own lives, and they can positively or negatively affect the lives of others. Rational adults can engage in self-evaluation and in the evaluation of others, evaluations that can affect future choices. And they can give reasons, good reasons, for their judgments. These qualities are exhibited by rational adults, and they are, at least to our best knowledge, exhibited only by them. Taken together they define what it is to be a rational adult, and we value rational adults, that is, we give them inherent value, because of these qualities. It is often said that rational adults exhibit the qualities of personhood, so we shall restrict the expression "person" to this limited class of human beings.

We also extend inherent value to other nonrational human beings, such as children, the senile, the mentally ill, and the handicapped, not merely because they are "look alikes," but also because they are potentially persons. They have emotions, are capable of interests, feel pain, and sometimes even exhibit a modicum of choice. But they do not exhibit enough rationality and self-awareness that one can attribute to them full adulthood and the opportunity for free choice.

Human beings are valued, then, just because they are human. Whatever unique qualities distinguish human beings, or in the more restricted case, persons, are very precious and should be safeguarded at all costs. Whatever prevents human beings from satisfying their basic needs and interests, whatever causes them pain, lessens the value of life. For persons, whatever interferes with their choices and actions violates their dignity and autonomy as rational adults. Thus whatever it is that violates humanhood or personhood is to abhored and rejected.

Another way to put this is that every human being has certain very basic rights. Basic moral rights derive from those qualities that uniquely characterize human beings, and in a more restricted context, rational adults. Conversely, basic moral rights are those characteristics of human beings and persons the absence of respect or exercise of which allow treatment that violates what is uniquely characteristic of human beings or persons. So for example, the right to life and the right not to be tortured are basic moral rights of all humans since without respect for life or pain human existence would be intolerable. The right to freedom is a basic moral right of rational adults since without being able to exercise choice, persons cannot develop themselves as persons. These rights are so fundamental and inviolable that every human being possesses them despite his or her particular social, political, historical, or even cultural situation. They should be respected and be able to be exercised everywhere, even at the expense of some allegedly practical interests.

The reader will notice that there are a number of assumptions to be cleared up in this definition. We must distinguish between possessing a right and having that right respected, and between possessing a right and being able to exercise it. We must ask whether or not all rights are absolute rights, and we must examine the relationship, if any, between legal rights and moral rights. We shall explore these ideas in the sections to follow. The reader will also notice that in the foregoing paragraphs we have made some assumptions that seem intuitively correct but are hard, perhaps impossible, to prove. We have assumed that human beings have value just because they are human. Moreover, we have assumed that personhood is limited to a restricted number of human beings, those who are rational adults, and that in addition to rationality, personhood includes freedom of choice and independence or autonomy. That is, (1) persons can truly make at least limited choices based on real alternatives, (2) freedom is unique to persons, and (3) freedom and personal autonomy are of great value. That rational adults or persons are truly free and can exercise choices will be left for another volume. That freedom is of inherent value cannot be proven, but it is an inherently plausible position. For readers who do not value human freedom, the arguments to follow will not be useful.

Personal Preferences, Legal Rights, and Moral Rights

A moral right is not merely a statement of personal preference. When I say, "I have a right to privacy," I am not merely expressing a personal desire to be left alone. I am arguing that "in principle" I am entitled to personal autonomy, and that there are many ways to justify or validate the principle to which I am appealing. One way to defend one's right is through appeal to the law. Legal rights are stated in rules, laws, or constitutional systems. Sometimes legal rights are claims made on the basis of an interpretation of the law—that is, what *should* be entailed by such rules or legal systems. Thus my privacy may be legally justified by appealing to our constitution even though the right to privacy is not explicitly stated in that document. Many rights are defined and defended by laws. The difficulty is that the laws that define or imply rights are not always just or fitting laws. Indeed, we must often use other principles in order to justify or criticize a certain rule or law. Conversely, not all moral principles we espouse are protected by legal codes. For example, in South Africa it is against the law to pay white persons and nonwhites equally for equal work. Most of us think this is an unjust law, and our reason for thinking this is that the law does not respect the rights of all South Africans equally. But to criticize this law one must appeal to some principle other than legality since in South Africa one *has* the legal right to pay equal work unequally. And it will not suffice merely to compare South African and United States legal codes on this matter, for what is to say that our laws are more valid than those of South Africa. One needs another, more general, principle to make this comparison. Moral rights are principles or standards to which one may appeal in evaluating laws, legal systems, or legally granted rights.

Rights, or at least basic rights, are sometimes called natural rights. A natural right is a right that is neither conventional nor institutional. It can neither be created nor artifically conferred, but is a right that everyone possesses just because he or she is human. Natural rights were once thought to be God-given or somehow genetically instilled in the nature of human beings, but such a view, as one can imagine, arouses many controversies about the nature of persons, our relation to God, etc., controversies that are important but with which we cannot deal in this essay. Thus natural rights are simply called human rights.

The term "human right," too, is controversial for two reasons. First, some philosphers hold that animals, like humans, have rights, that is, animal rights. But the term "human right" sometimes is interpreted to mean that all and only humans have rights, thus excluding animals from having any rights, even so-called animal rights. Second, the term "human right" sounds like some entitlement everyone *in fact* has. But this is not quite accurate. There is a literal sense in which not every person on this planet has a *recognized* entitlement because there are places where these rights are not respected. Human rights are moral or normative rights as distinct from legal rights, for although they are rights that all individuals possess equally because of their humanity, they are not in fact always respected as they should be. They are rights everyone everywhere possesses, despite peculiar local customs or laws, but they are rights that are not universally recognized, honored, or allowed exercise. Thus human rights are best called moral rights. Some of these are basic moral rights, that is, rights that are inherently characteristic of human beings or persons and that are the basis for all other rights claims.

CHARACTERISTICS OF MORAL RIGHTS

There are a number of important distinctions that need to be made in describing moral rights. One must distinguish (a) between active and passive rights, (b) between positive and negative rights, and (c) between absolute and prima facie rights. Moreover, all moral rights have at least three characteristics: (1) all moral rights are equal rights; (2) all moral rights are universal rights; and (3) moral rights have an obligatory character. These distinctions and characteristics will obviously apply to basic moral rights, since all basic moral rights are moral rights, although not all moral rights are basic moral rights. Let us discuss these.

Active and Passive Rights

To understand the distinction between possessing a right and honoring or exercising it, it is helpful to distinguish between passive rights and active rights. A passive right is a right that requires recognition by others and sometimes action by another person. Rights to life, for example, are passive rights because they require the recognition and protection by other persons or institutions in order that life be respected. Thus passive rights do not always entail action on the part of the rights claimant, and passive rights always entail second-party duties of others. Rights of nonpersons are passive rights since the "claimant" of the right in question cannot literally activate that claim. In order for nonrational human beings to have their rights protected, other persons must exercise their obligations to recognize and defend these rights.

The right to freedom, on the other hand, is an example of an active right, a right that requires positive action on the part of the rights claimant. One must do something, or be restrained from doing something, that is, make choices or be prevented from choosing, in order to exercise one's freedom. Another way to think of the distinction between active and passive rights is that an active right is a right to personal sovereignty over inviolable personal rights, liberties that have to do with what I can exercise and control: myself. Unlike passive rights, active rights require exercise by the rights claimant, so these rights are possessed only by rational adults.[3] Thus every human being possesses certain rights. Some of these are passive rights, rights that require recognition or protection by others to be realized. Others are active rights, rights that require exercise by the rights claimant and merely the nonintervention of others. These distinctions will be important in analyzing the moral character of rights.

[3]See Joel Feinberg, *Social Philosophy* (Englewood Cliffs, N.J.: Prentice-Hall, Inc., 1973), pp. 59–61.

Positive and Negative Rights

Connected with the notions of active and passive rights are the notions of positive and negative rights. A negative right is a right to be left alone or not interfered with in some way. The right not to be tortured, for example, is a negative right. Negative rights require little on the part of others except merely to respect noninterference. Positive rights, on the other hand, are rights *to* something and involve action on the part of others. The right to security is a positive right since it includes a right to protection and requires action on the part of others.

Both negative and positive rights may be active or passive. The right not to be tortured is a passive (negative) right, requiring no action on the part of the rights claimant. The right to be left alone, however, if extended to include the right to make choices as one pleases, includes the active component of having to exercise choice in order to realize that right. Similarly, positive rights may be passive rights, such as the right to security. Positive rights may also be active rights, the most propitious example of which is what is called the positive right to freedom, the right to be free to develop oneself, a right that both requires actions on my part and calls for others not merely to refrain from interfering but also to assist in my development. More will be said about the positive right to freedom in a later section.[4]

The distinction between positive and negative rights will be important to the subject matter of this book. A number of philosophers argue that only negative rights are candidates for universal moral rights, because only negative rights allow the maximum exercise of rights with minimum demands or restraints on the part of others. This allows maximum freedom, a most basic right. Positive rights, which require action on the part of others not merely to respect them but also to assist in their realization, infringe on one's right to be left alone by requiring active involvement in the achievement or the defense of the rights of another. Positive rights also infringe on the right of the claimant by requiring rights protection even when this is not desired by, or desirable to, that person, according to this view. For example, the right to subsistence, the right to have one's basic needs fulfilled, is a positive active right, because it demands not only positive action on the part of the rights claimant, but also requires all of us to help those in need who cannot help themselves. According to defenders of negative rights, this requirement infringes on the rights of those not in need to do what they please by forcing them to contribute to the needy, and it also infringes on the rights of the needy to control their own destiny.

In response other philosophers argue that the distribution of property, talents, resources, and accidents of birth or environment are such that unless positive rights are explicitly recognized some people will have none

[4]See Feinberg, pp. 12–17, 59–61, and 97–98 for further discussion.

of their rights respected and will not be able to exercise them. What is most interesting is that many advocates of negative rights also defend the right to private ownership, an active right that requires other persons to protect property claims against counterclaims or infringements. Later we shall try to show that the concept of a positive right need not be antithetical to the maximum exercise of rights, so long as the exercise of rights is conceived of as the exercise of equal rights.

Absolute Rights, Prima Facie Rights, and Rights Conflicts

A distinction is often drawn between indefeasible and defeasible rights. Indefeasible rights are of two sorts. First, a right might be an exceptionless right, a right that could never be overridden or outweighed no matter what circumstances prevailed. If the right to life, for example, is exceptionless, no one would ever be justified in taking another person's life, even in self-defense. It is obviously difficult to justify any right as an exceptionless right. Second, indefeasible rights might be absolute rights, rights that hold without exception within a restricted set of circumstances or for certain classes of persons. For example, H. L. A. Hart argues that the equal right to freedom is an absolute right for all rational adults. Ordinarily, according to Hart, there can be no valid exceptions to this right for this restricted class of human beings.[5] Although some moral rights might be absolute rights, most seem to be defeasible rights, or what are called prima facie rights. Prima facie rights are rights that can be set aside or overridden, but only in special cases and for good reasons. 'Good reasons' include (a) instances in which curtailing one person's rights is necessary because that person has violated or in all likelihood will violate the rights of others; (b) cases of conflicts between equal claims to exercise the same right; and/or (c) cases in which two equal rights conflict and where both cannot be respected or exercised.

The first set of instances, (a), obviously refers to persons who exhibit criminal behavior, that is, persons who violate the right to life or restrict the freedoms of others by their activities. One then has the right to curtail their exercise of rights in order to respect the rights of those violated. The offender still possesses her rights, but she is kept from exercising them. Second, (b), there are also instances when there are conflicts of the same right, for example in some childbirth cases when one must choose between saving the mother and saving the unborn child. In these cases one right must be sacrificed or neither mother nor child will survive. How one chooses is always subject to debate. One might plausibly argue that to save the mother, who presumably is a rational adult, is preferable, all things considered, since she is a fully developed person. But the choice is not an

---

[5]H. L. A. Hart, "Are There Any Natural Rights?," *Philosophical Review*, 64 (1955), p. 176.

easy one, because the unborn child has the potentiality of personhood as well. In the third set of cases, (c), conflicts arise when two different but equal rights conflict, say freedom and national security in a time of war. It is sometimes argued that one may temporarily override freedom for the sake of national security, but only during the war period. These conflicts are the hardest to resolve, because one chooses between two different kinds of rights.

Sometime in conflicts between prima facie rights one may make compromises that, while imperfect, respect in a limited way the rights of both parties. For example, we incarcerate criminals, but lately there has been an attempt to extend to prisoners some sorts of rights, albeit not the right to freedom. More will be said about the resolution of rights conflicts through compromise in Part One when we discuss the Manville Corporation. Notice that in all cases of conflicts of rights the justice of overriding any right will involve considerations about the moral rights of others, not merely the power or prejudices of another person or institution.

The Equality of Rights

All moral rights are equal rights, that is, (1) every person has and possesses every right equally, so that (2) every person is entitled to the respect or the exercise of every moral right, and that equally with everyone else. Because moral rights are nonconventional, this equality holds independently of sex, skin color, religious beliefs, places of birth, or present circumstances. For example, a black worker in South Africa has different *legal* rights than a white worker. But both persons possess the same equal *moral* rights, and the moral rights they possess are the same as those of black or white workers in, say, Chicago. And workers in Chicago possess the same moral rights as, say, their employer, even though the employer hires and pays them. A South African's exercise of freedom is, or should be, equal to mine. The reason for this is obvious. If rights were not equal in the sense that one could grant moral rights to everyone and yet defend their unequal recognition or exercise, then one could argue that blacks and whites in South Africa both possess rights, such as the right to freedom, but that whites for some reason deserve more of some right, that is, that they are entitled to exercise more freedom than nonwhites.

The notion of the equality of rights must be further qualified. In exercising a moral right or in respecting (or violating) a right of another, one has to take into account not merely the equality of rights as equally *possessed* by everyone, but also the application of the notion of "equality" in that particular situation. That is, in recognizing and exercising moral rights, one does not appeal literally to the idea of equal rights to "equal treatment," but rather to the notion of the right to equal consideration or "treatment as an equal." Let us see what this entails.

The right to equal consideration is a controversial notion not so much because of its content, which I shall analyze in the next paragraphs, but because it is not clear whether the right to equal consideration is a basic moral right, the most basic of all rights, or an extension of the definition of moral rights as equal rights, an extension necessary when describing the equality of rights when they are being recognized, exercised or adjudicated. We shall not decide that question in this book. In any case, the notion of equal consideration, whether or not it is a separate basic moral right, is crucial to understanding the idea of equal rights, and it is this, not its place in the ontology of rights, that is of importance to the theses of this book.

The equality of rights implies that if there are any rights at all, part of their character is that every one is entitled to equal consideration of a specific right. Some contemporary philosophers such as Ronald Dworkin argue that equal consideration defines the ways in which individual rights should be respected or exercised in particular situations. Dworkin's point is this. In applying a theory of (equal) moral rights in particular cases, one is not, in fact, saying that one should recognize every right in the same way in every situation, or that everyone should unrestrictively be able to exercise any right equally with anyone else's exercise of that right. Rather, Dworkin is arguing that every person has the right to be treated as an equal in that rights claim.

> The right to treatment as an equal must be taken to be fundamental . . . and that the more restrictive right to equal treatment holds only in those special circumstances in which , . . it follows from the more fundamental right.[6]

In other words, in fair procedures, equals are to be treated equally, and unequals are to be afforded more or less consideration in order to equalize their position.

Dworkin illustrates this point with the following example. Suppose a mother has two children, one of whom is very ill, and she has money for medicine for only one child. To be fair, she does not divide the medicine equally because the healthy child is in an unequally better position healthwise than the ill one. The mother *considers* each equally, but to respect the equal rights of both she gives the medicine to the sick child. Similarly, in hiring one does not distribute jobs equally. This would be considered unfair, because some persons are more qualified than others for a particular job, and some persons simply are incapable of performing certain tasks for which, if jobs were distributed equally, they might be hired. To be fair to all applicants, one considers each application equally, eliminating considerations that are irrelevant for the job, such as whether the applicant is black, a woman, etc. Then one evaluates qualifications for the job in question. If there was equal distribution in hiring, for example, I could demand a job

---

[6]Ronald Dworkin, *Taking Rights Seriously* (Cambridge: Harvard University Press, 1977), p. 273.

with the Chicago Bears, or my lawyer husband could become a medical doctor. If there was no equal consideration, on the other hand, I could be turned down for a professorship because I am a woman, or my husband could be barred from practice because his wife worked.

Similarly, in exercising an active right, every person should be able to exercise that right equally. But this is not equivalent to the "equal exercise" of a right. The criminal, for example, has the right to exercise her freedom equally with other criminals, but not the right to equal exercise since in the latter instance she tries to exercise her freedom to the detriment of the freedom of others.

While the notion of equality is fundamental to moral rights, in settling particular rights issues it is equal consideration, not equal treatment as such, that is the most fundamental basis for settling the question. In summary, this means that (a) everyone possesses rights equally. Further, (b) the concept of equal rights demands equal respect for every right. This should be interpreted to mean that all humans should be respected or treated as equals, not that every human being deserves equal respect when that results in unequal treatment. Finally, (c) the notion of equal rights allows the exercise of each right equally. If my exercise of a right interferes with your right to equal exercise, this violates your right and my actions must be moderated or restrained accordingly to balance both exercises. Thus the equality of rights requires equal consideration or the right to treatment as an equal in recognizing, exercising, or adjudicating rights and rights claims.

The Universality of Moral Rights

Moral rights are universal rights. One test of whether a given rights claim should be understood as affirming a moral right is to ask whether one is prepared to universalize one's claim. What is meant by "universalize" is simply that when one is said to possess a moral right, it is understood that *every* person must be conceived to possess that right and to possess it equally, and that that right should be universally respected or allowed equal exercise. In the next section I shall argue that if a claim to rights cannot meet this universality requirement, that is, if one is unwilling to recognize that *all* persons possess the right one claims for oneself, and possess that right equally, then the so-called right one contends to have is not a moral right. What is important here is to understand that the definition of a moral right requires not merely that the right be possessed by everyone, everywhere, but also that it should be respected and exercised everywhere. Thus one may appeal to this notion of universality in evaluating particular situations where one thinks that rights are violated.

Rights and Obligations

Because moral rights are possessed universally even if they are not universally recognized, they become the basis for claims to entitlements, and sometimes for claims against some person or institution as well. Worries about rights, then, will naturally arise in a social context. Because moral rights are often claims against others, and because rights are normative, one person's rights are often connected with the obligations or the duties of other persons. Because of this connection between rights and the obligations of others (second-party duties) it has been contended that "when one person has a moral right, some other person or persons have corresponding obligations."[7]

Some philosophers contend that *every* right is defined by, or at least correlated in some way with, a duty of other persons.[8] But there are exceptions to this thesis. For example, if two equally qualified persons apply for a job, both may have an equal right to that job, but if the employer has only one position available, she has no obligation to hire both. Conversely, one may feel an obligation to contribute to a charitable organization such as the Crusade of Mercy, but that organization does not necessarily have a correlative *right* to that contribution. Furthermore, recalling our discussion of active and passive rights, a passive right entails second-party duties on the part of others to honor and protect that right, but an active right merely requires the negative duty not to interfere. Consequently the notion of relationship of rights to second-party duties is not as important in describing active rights.

Because of the shortcomings of the rights-duties thesis in the examples cited above and when applied to active rights, an alternative is to appeal to the notion of the universalizability of moral rights to account for their obligatory character, since to identify a moral right one must confirm the universality and equal application of that right.[9] For example, it is commonly claimed that every person possesses the right to freedom. To make a rational argument for this entitlement, one must grant that the right to freedom is an equal right and a universal moral right. Every adult person possesses and should be able to exercise his freedom equally. Therefore, if I claim this right, I should respect not merely the fact that everyone possesses this right, but also the exercise of this right equally by others. This is an obligation that is inherent in my claim to the exercise of freedom because to deny this obligation would be equivalent to denying the universality of that right. Then I would be saying that I can exercise freedom but that some others cannot, or cannot exercise it as an equal right. I might *want* to argue this way, but it makes my claim to freedom very

[7]See Richard Brandt, *Ethical Theory* (Englewood Cliffs, N.J.: Prentice-Hall, Inc., 1959), especially p. 436.

[8]Jeremy Bentham was probably the originator of this view. See *An Introduction to the Principles of Morals and Legislation* from the *Collected Works of Jeremy Bentham* (University of London: Athlone Press, 1970).

[9]See for example, Alan Gewirth, *Reason and Morality* (Chicago: University of Chicago Press, 1978), especially Chapters 2 and 3; and Patricia H. Werhane, "The Obligatory Nature of Moral Rights," American Philosophical Association Western Division Meetings, Detroit, Michigan, April 29, 1980.

questionable. For suppose that someone interferes with my freedom. If I do not recognize the universality of freedom I cannot object to this interference. I cannot object because my original contention was that I have the right to exercise freedom, but others do not or do not equally. More generally, the universality or universalizability of any moral rights claim involves obligations to respect equally the rights and the exercise of rights of others. This kind of first-party obligatory character is built into the nature of active moral rights.

CANDIDATES FOR BASIC MORAL RIGHTS

What are some candidates for basic moral rights? What qualities must be recognized and exercised to assure humanhood, and in the more restricted sense, personhood, and what sorts of things, if denied, would violate them? Theorists debate endlessly as to what is *the* most basic right. We cannot settle that debate, but we can examine a number of very basic rights, the absence of which would make human life as we value it abhorent or even impossible. It will turn out that there are two sorts of basic rights, those that all human beings have, and a more limited number (one or two) that only rational adults or persons possess.

The Right to Equal Consideration

Earlier we argued that equal consideration was a crucial element in defining the equal recognition and exercise of rights. There we acknowledged that the right to equal consideration might be the most basic right, or it might merely be part of the definition of moral rights. Its ontological status in the family of rights will not be decided here, but its importance for the discussion of rights cannot be exaggerated.

The Right to Security and Subsistence

In a recent book, *Basic Rights,* Henry Shue argues that security and subsistence are the most basic rights. About these rights Shue says,

> Security and subsistence are basic rights . . . because of the roles they play in both the enjoyment and the protection of all other rights. Other rights could not be enjoyed in the absence of security or subsistence, even if the other rights were somehow miraculously protected in such a situation. And other rights could in any case not be protected if security or subsistence could credibly be threatened.[10]

According to Shue, then, security and subsistence are most basic because life, freedom, and even equal opportunity could not be realized in any society where security or subsistence were not protected.

[10]Henry Shue, *Basic Rights* (Princeton: Princeton University Press, 1980), p. 30.

One cannot deny Shue's point that security and subsistence are very basic rights since, as he points out, without them human life is virtually unbearable. Whether or not they are more basic than freedom or life is a question for debate. In any case, in particular applications of those rights one would want to emphasize that Shue's candidates for basic rights are equal rights, that is, every person has an *equal* right to security and subsistence, a point that is assumed in Shue's theory.

The Right to Life and The Right Not to Be Tortured

Some philosophers argue that the right to life is most basic because without *that* talking about human rights would be superfluous. Others argue that the right not to be tortured or enslaved is most basic, because *human* existence is simply intolerable where slavery or torture is permitted. It is beyond the scope of this book to make a definitive case for one or more of these rights. Needless to say, without equal consideration, security and subsistence, or freedom from torture or enslavement, human life as it is valued would be impossible. All of the rights we have listed are therefore basic moral rights. They are also passive rights, rights that should be recognized everywhere for all human beings, and that need to be recognized or honored by others.

The Right to Freedom

Let us now discuss a right possessed only by rational adults, the right to freedom. The right to freedom is surely one of the most basic rights, and a right that is of considerable importance in our society. It is usually defined as a prima facie right because there are instances when it can be overridden with justification, as in times of national security. There are many definitions of freedom. We shall consider only a few that will be important for our later analysis.

A. *Freedom of choice and action*   As H. L. A. Hart notices, freedom is ordinarily considered a valid entitlement only for "any adult human being capable of choice,"[11] that is, for any rational person who can be held responsible for his or her actions. Children, the insane, the senile, and other persons who are so mentally handicapped that they cannot make free choices are precluded from this right, since to claim the right one must personally exercise or be capable of exercising it, capable, that is, of acting or trying to act freely. Notice that this definition of freedom identifies freedom with freedom of choice and action.

Hart urges that the equal right to freedom is an absolute right of restricted application to the class of all rational autonomous adults. It is the most basic right, according to Hart, because it forms the grounds upon

[11]H. L. A. Hart, "Are There Any Natural Rights?," *Philosophical Review*, 64 (1955), p. 176.

which one assumes that autonomous human beings may make rights claims and recognize and exercise their duties. One cannot be said to have obligations to respect the rights of others unless one is free and capable of doing so. Freedom in this sense, then, is the necessary condition for the recognition of rights and their obligations. Freedom is the prerequisite for the realization of other moral rights. Notice, however, that because freedom is a basic moral right only for rational adults, it is a necessary condition only for the realization of other *active* rights. It is not the most basic right for all human beings, since those who are not persons or rational adults and cannot exercise freedom still possess certain rights.

   B. *Freedom as autonomy: freedom and privacy*   Connected with freedom of choice is the notion of freedom as autonomy. In order to make free choices, one must be at least somewhat independent, that is, one must be treated as an individual separate from other persons. Freedom in this sense is related to personal privacy, since to be autonomous at least part of one's self must be kept private to oneself. If one's personal life, one's thoughts and feelings become public and are not sacrosanct, one is no longer independent, one is not able to exercise personal autonomy, and one cannot be said to be free or to have a right to freedom.

   C. *Negative and positive freedom*   In the foregoing definitions, freedom might mean simply the right not to be coerced, the right to be let alone, or the right not to be forced into involuntary behavior.[12] This is a negative right, a privilege that does not necessarily require any positive action on the part of others except that they simply leave everyone to themselves. This is an important notion in business, because corporations argue that they have the right to be left alone to do as they please and that this includes the right to make mutually voluntary agreements without being coerced by laws or government. It is hard to imagine that we do not have this negative right not to be coerced, since without it voluntary behavior, and thus autonomous choices and actions, would be impossible. One must remember, however, that this is an *equal* right. Everyone possesses it equally, and every person should be able to exercise it equally notwithstanding the proviso that it is not "equal exercise" but rather the concept of "exercising freedom equally" that is at stake.

   Sometimes freedom is defined as a positive right. In that definition freedom is ". . . the desire of the individual to be his own master . . . to be self-directed, . . . to be moved by his own conscious purposes . . . to act and decide rather than be acted upon and decided for by others."[13] This defini-

   [12]Isaiah Berlin, "Two Concepts of Liberty," *Four Essays on Liberty* (Oxford: Oxford University Press, 1969, rpt. 1975), pp. 122–131. Excerpt reprinted by permission of Oxford University Press. See also Eric Mack, "Natural and Contractual Rights," *Ethics*, 87 (1977), pp. 152–59.

   [13]Berlin, p. 131 and C. B. MacPherson, "Berlin's Division of Liberty," *Democratic Theory* (Oxford: Clarendon Press, 1973), p. 108.

tion of freedom has been offered by many philosophers to take into account the fact that merely having autonomy, the right not to be coerced or the right to be left alone, is not enough in itself to ensure the development of freedom for every person. The negative right to freedom is a passive right unless opportunities for positive enjoyment of autonomy and self-development are linked to it, because by itself it merely leaves people alone to do as they please so long as they do not infringe on the rights of others to be left alone too. In that scenario some will be more aggressive than others and exercise their freedom to the neglect of those who find themselves in less propitious circumstances. For example, at the outset of the industrial revolution adults were not literally forced into working in a factory. Jobs at certain wages were offered, persons were "free" to accept or not accept these offers, and workers could quit at any time. However, the economic climate in the nineteenth century was such both in Europe and later in the United States that in order to survive one had to work and the only jobs available were factory jobs at menial wages under wretched working conditions. Even in a political society espousing the negative right to freedom, economic conditions virtually dictated that persons take these jobs. In these circumstances a negative right to freedom was not enough, by itself, to assure the positive noncoercive development of every person, guaranteeing that he or she could truly act as an autonomous human being. The negative right to freedom, then, does not allow everyone to exercise their rights equally, since one person's exercise of liberty may restrict the liberty of another, because it damages the other's freedom or because not all persons have equal opportunities to develop the direction of their lives.

According to defenders of a positive right to freedom, one is not free unless everyone can actually exercise their freedom, and exercise it equally. While positive liberty, at least according to one interpretation, includes the right "to participate in the process by which my life is to be controlled,"[14] it is also claimed that "the only sensible way to measure individual liberty is to measure the aggregate net liberty of all the individuals in a given society."[15] In an unequal society, that is, a society where not everyone can exercise their choices and control their lives to the same extent, one is required to restrain one's own freedom and assist others to develop theirs. According to this view, so long as some persons are not equally free, everyone's right to do as they please is restrained by this requirement.

What is interesting for the purposes of this book is that a definition of the right to freedom as a negative right has by and large been adopted by those who espouse a laissez-faire (free enterprise) economy. And the definition is often appealed to, albeit questionably, to defend the absolute right of productive organizations to do as they please even when their actions

[14]Ibid.
[15]MacPherson, p. 117.

might conflict with the rights of others. The definition of freedom as a positive right is often propounded by theorists who defend a more regulated or even a socialist economic system. This notion of freedom is sometimes used, also questionably, to support control and even government ownership of productive organizations in order to equalize and promote the self-development of each individual in a society.

What both views often neglect is that *any* right to freedom is equally possessed and should be able to be exercised equally by everyone. The alleged rights of productive organizations to do as they please must be seen in the context of the equal rights of individuals affected by organizational decisions. Conversely, the positive right to self-development, too, is a right to be exercised equally. If assisting others to develop themselves unduly interferes with the exercise of one's own freedom, this too, is coercive.

How should freedom be defined? Freedom includes the right to autonomy, the right to be left alone, and the right not to be coerced. These are necessary for the exercise of free choice. But the inability to act independently or autonomously to direct the course of one's life should be recognized as a form of "coercion." Therefore the notion of freedom must include equal opportunities to exercise self-development. Moreover, given the obligatory nature of active moral rights, each of us has a duty to restrain our own exercise of freedom when it interferes with the equal exercise of the freedom of another. Thus one cannot ignore persons who cannot exercise their own freedoms without bringing one's own moral right to freedom into question, since so long as the unequal exercise of freedoms prevails, the ideal of moral rights as equal rights is not realized. Thus everyone has an obligation, an obligation derived from their demand for freedom as a moral right, to assist in providing equal opportunities for those unable to exercise their freedom equally. Later it will be argued that this sort of freedom is an ideal that is realizable in a free enterprise economy such as our own. But freedom should not be extended to include positive requirements to assist others when this overrides one's own equal exercise of autonomy. A balance must be struck.

The Right to Private Ownership

The concept of a moral right is consistent with theories of capitalism, since standard defenses of that economic theory assume that all persons have certain rights, including, in particular, a right we have not mentioned, the right to private ownership. Private ownership is important in a capitalist economy such as our own. In theory, at least, it separates economic and political power by placing property and capital, thus economic control, in the hands of private citizens. This, in turn, serves as a balance to political power, which needs a strong economy to realize its aims. Private ownership allows privately held businesses, such as corporations, to develop as independent productive organizations. The way in which private ownership develops in a free-enterprise system in turn affects the nature of the employee-employer exchange in such economies. Employers, e.g. entrepreneurs and corporations, own property such as land, factories, advertising agencies, banks, and the like, and they are thus in a position to hire people and to pay them. Employees develop the production of their employer, and their employer in return (again in theory) pays the employee for his or her contribution. Thus, much of employment in a free-enterprise economy depends on privately owned businesses. In the philosophical literature on ownership and property rights there is a myriad of justifications for this right. And, in return, critics of capitalism argue against the viability or the justice of private ownership. All of these arguments and counterarguments are interesting, but there is not the space to consider them here.

For the sake of arguments in this book, we shall assume that it is not contradictory to a theory of moral rights to claim that every person has an equal right to private ownership. It must be acknowledged, however, that private ownership is not on a par with the most basic rights we have discussed in preceding sections. This is because one could live fully as a human being and develop freely as a person without the right to private ownership so long as one lived in a communal society where no one had that right, or where everyone shared all properties fully and equally. Private ownership, then, is a conventional right strongly held by certain societies. In some of these societies, such as our own, it is often held that private ownership is a *moral* right because of its role in balancing political and economic power, and because of its connection with the right to freedom. Let us see why this is so.

Private ownership in most capitalist economic systems is defined as the right to buy, sell, and own material properties, including capital, land, factories, goods, and services. Private ownership is a *right* because it entitles one to own something in such a way that he or she is protected against others wishing to own that property, and protected from infringements on that property. Ownership, then, entails at least a three-term relation between the claimant—the owner or prospective owner, the property claimed, and others who are in a position to make a claim or infringe on that right. Later, in Chapter Eight, we will suggest that because some property ownership allows the owner to offer employment, property rights sometimes involve a fourth relationship, that between owner and employees.

Notice that private ownership is both a positive and an active right. The right to property is a right to something, and one must exercise that right, for example buy, sell or own property, in order to have it recognized. Second, in our society at least, private ownership depends on a right to freedom, that is, the negative right to do as one pleases so long as that does not infringe on the rights of others. This is because the right to private ownership includes the right freely to buy, sell, or exchange property within normal market restrictions.

What we wish to show is that a private enterprise economic system that recognizes private ownership as a moral right is not antithetical to individual liberty, in particular the freedom to develop autonomously one's own life. Strong private economic organizations do not necessarily preclude the existence of justice and fairness so long as the equal rights of every person are recognized and enforced. If all of this can be demonstrated, and I think it can, then our assumption that private ownership is not contradictory to the recognition and development of basic moral rights will not be unfounded.

POLITICAL AND ECONOMIC RIGHTS

In discussions of moral rights a distinction is sometimes made between political rights and economic rights. Political rights are rights propounded to establish a just political state. The right to life, the rights to freedom of speech, assembly, movement and the press, the right to due process and a fair trial, the right to equal opportunity, and the right to vote, are all political rights. They are rights that adjudicate decisions when the public interest or public policy is at stake. One of the questions we shall ask in Part Two is whether or not these rights also hold in private relationships between persons or between persons and productive organizations. Political rights are sometimes contrasted with economic rights, which are rights bound up with survival, subsistence, labor and ownership. The distinction is not altogether clear. The right to life, a vital political right, is connected with survival and subsistence. And the rights to equal opportunity and private ownership are important both politically and economically. Keeping this in mind, the essay shall describe some important employer and employee political rights in the workplace, for example, the rights to free expression, to due process, and to privacy. Because productive organizations in our society, such as corporations, make claims to political rights, it is important to see whether and how these may be justified and how these claims coincide or clash with employee political rights entitlements in the workplace. I shall also discuss some important economic rights of employees, the rights to safety, to fair pay, and to participation in the workplace, but will pay little attention to some other important rights, such as the rights to life, to equal opportunity, and to work. We shall assume, for the sake of the argument that the latter are valid moral claims that should be recognized everywhere, but I shall not prove that this is the case. This omission is somewhat justified because economic rights to survival, to work, and to equal opportunity have been widely discussed in the literature on employment, while other rights of employees in the workplace have been very much neglected.

RIGHTS AND INTERESTS

A strong theory of moral rights asserts that there are certain rights human beings possess everywhere, and in any culture, no matter what. Such a position is often criticized as being too radical, too idealistic, or too stringent, because it does not take into account human needs and interests, the frailties of human nature, or the contingencies of particular historical or economic situations. For example, to espouse the right to freedom in a country such as Cambodia ignores the realities of a situation where bare survival—the satisfaction of the most basic needs, not rights, is the primary concern. If basic needs are not met, human rights are not at issue at all.

Sometimes the defense or enforcement of an individual right in a particular circumstance may not be in the best interests of a community. One of the issues for debate in our present legal system, for example, is the alleged rights of the accused. It is often pointed out that when known felons or murderers are freed because their rights were violated during arrest or trial this undermines the ideal purpose of moral rights, which should be to fulfill human interests. The safety of the community in these instances, it is argued, is forfeited to protect the rights of a few persons who little deserve such protection and, in the process, the rights of victims and possible victims are threatened. In business these same sorts of arguments flourish. Morally questionable acts of productive organizations are sometimes forgiven if they serve the economic interests of the community. For example, it is sometimes contended that environmental rights must be sacrificed to insure economic well-being, or that bribery in foreign countries to meet the competition is permissible if it is an accepted practice there.

Arguments that justify the recognition and exercise of moral rights on the basis of human interests are often called utilitarian arguments. Utilitarian justifications of these sorts are very convincing, and one does not want to defend a theory of moral rights that creates or abets harms. However, some utilitarian defenses of human action may raise issues more problematic than the rights theses they are meant to attack. Some utilitarians assert that any action is a good action if, on balance, it satisfies a majority of needs or human interests, others if it promotes or maximizes human happiness or, at the least, reduces pain. The first challenge to such a position is to ask whether a simple majority is enough to justify an action. Of course utilitarians respond that one must measure the quality as well as the quantity of needs and interests. For example, ordinarily one cannot justify murdering someone even if that act would produce some positive benefit for a great number of people. The harm to that one person is measured as much greater than any positive benefit to others.

Many utilitarians contend that "no act of harming another person can be justified by reference to the benefit of others",[16] or more restrictively, that no act of harming another person that reduces his or her *freedom* can be justified even if it benefits others.[17] At best, according to this view, harming someone can only be justified when the act prevents similar harm to the freedom of a large number of persons. But utilitarians disagree on these points. If the sacrifice of one life would save the lives of say, a thousand persons, would such an act be justified? Some utilitarians argue that an action is justified only if it produces some positive benefits *and* does not create any harms, but others might support the sacrifice.

One group of utilitarians, "rule utilitarians," says that an action must be judged on the basis of the rule that action exemplifies. One evaluates the rule not the act, but on the basis of whether or not that rule, if followed, would in the long run maximize happiness or some other good. According to this view, a particular act is a right action if the rule or principle it exemplifies, if followed, would generate a balance or maximization of good.

The danger in using needs, interests, or happiness to evaluate human actions is that even when judgments are based on universal rules one might conceivably justify an action or a general rule for actions that is overwhelmingly in the interest of the vast majority but that nevertheless causes irreparable harm to the basic moral rights of some person or group of persons.[18]

Recently the well-known philosopher Richard Brandt put forth a more complicated utilitarian theory of rights. In brief, according to Brandt, to say that X has a moral right to Y is to say

> It is *justified* for people in X's society to be strongly motivated, overridingly so normally . . . and to disapprove others who are not so motivated, to enable X . . . to do, have or enjoy Y primarily because of the failure of others to have this motivation, and . . . it is justified for him to take reasonable steps of protest, calculated to encourage others to have the motivation to enable anyone in a similar situation to do, have, or enjoy things like Y.[19]

Two elements are important to notice in Brandt's lengthy definition of a moral right. First, the motivation and the justification for people in X's society to support X's right are overriding interests that they share, that they defend, that they embody in a moral code, and that they will even

---

[16]Jan Narveson, *Morality and Utility* (Baltimore: Johns Hopkins Press, 1967), p. 161.

[17]See John Stuart Mill, *Essay on Liberty* (New York: Meridian Books, 1968).

[18]For a fuller discussion of this criticism of utilitarianism see H. J. McCloskey, "A Note on Utilitarian Punishment," *Mind,* 72 (1963). For its defense see J. J. C. Smart, "An Outline of a System of Utilitarian Ethics," in Smart and Bernard Williams, *Utilitarianism, For and Against* (Cambridge: Cambridge University Press, 1976).

[19]Richard Brandt, "The Concept of a Moral Right and its Function," *Journal of Philosophy,* 80 (1983), p. 40.

fight for, according to Brandt. Second, part of the justificatory motivation is that the right is an interest that can be realized. Brandt says in this regard that

> One implication of the definition . . . is that there can be no moral right, not even a prima facie right, to Y in a society where there is no possibility of any person or group of persons in the society enabling X (and others with equal rights) to have Y.[20]

Now this view is interesting because it relates moral rights to human motivation and to overriding societal interests, which a society will defend because it recognizes the diversity of rights espoused in different cultures, and because it implicitly suggests the ways in which rights evolve in different cultures. But the recognition and exercise of moral rights, according to this theory, are limited to realizable overriding societal interests. That is, moral rights are identified as rights that are recognized, exercised, and defended, or that could be recognized and exercised and would be defended in that society. But by this analysis what is a justified moral right in one society may not be a right at all in another. Thus this position does not entirely account for the universality of basic moral rights, that is, that basic moral rights are possessed by everyone everywhere, a characteristic I take to be their ultimate test. Brandt recognizes that there could be some "world-wide" rights, rights that are of universal interest and that conceivably could be realized everywhere. But these are not universal rights in the sense that everyone everywhere possesses them even if no one recognizes or exercises them. According to Brandt's position, one could have a world-wide moral code in which the overriding motivations and interests expressed would be such that enslaving a small group of persons could, in certain extreme circumstances, be justfiable if it greatly benefited a large community.[21] This treatment could be applied equally, say, to all physically handicapped twenty-four year old males with green eyes. However such a code, even if agreed upon world-wide and defended universally, would not respect the basic moral rights of one small group of human beings, in particular their right to freedom. And since according to this theory there are no universal moral rights that everyone possesses even when they are not respected or exercised, there would be no higher principle to which to appeal, i.e., universal rights, to evaluate the rights or absence of rights of this small minority under this world-wide code.

Returning to criticisms of rights theories, some are valid criticisms, but they apply particular interpretations of defenses of moral rights. For

---

[20]Brandt, p. 41. He says further, 'a right' implies 'can. . .' So if a society cannot realize a right, persons in that society do not have that right.

[21]I heard Brandt defend this view at the InterAmerican Congress of Philosophy, Florida State University, October 1981. See also his book, *A Theory of the Good and the Right* (Oxford: Clarendon Press, 1979), especially pp. 306–26.

example, one cannot preempt survival for the right to freedom in places such as Cambodia. But many rights theorists such as Shue argue that the right to subsistence, not the right to freedom, is the most basic human right. Other theorists point out that survival without respect for rights, living as a slave for example, is not human survival at all.

In thinking about the rights of accused persons, we have in this country in different periods in our history tended to espouse certain principles at the expense of others. In the 1950s and 1960s we took up the cause of the rights of accused persons in reaction to the traditional absolute disregard of the fact that accused persons are *persons* and have rights even if they were guilty of heinous crimes. However, in our zeal we sometimes forgot that all rights are equal rights. Victims or possible victims have rights too, and should be able to exercise them so that one set cannot be upheld at the expense of the other. Similarly in business until recently it was felt that corporations had almost absolute rights to do what they pleased. In reaction to this we have overregulated business, and we have taken up the causes of consumer, environmental, and employee rights. Some proponents of the latter now seem to argue that only citizens, consumers and employees, but not employers, have legitimate rights claims. So the notion that rights are *equal* rights has, as in other cases, been ignored.

In what follows we shall adopt the view that universally every person possesses moral rights. These are to be conceived of as equal rights, as I shall remind the reader repeatedly. Rights claims are always entitlements to *equal* respect or *equal* exercise, and in evaluating rights one must always try to balance one set of claims against other *equal* demands. In many instances theses will be defended on utilitarian grounds as well. But it shall be repeatedly contended that in the last analysis rights claims overrule utilitarian arguments because if they do not, one might justify harms to individuals on the basis of some questionable benefit. Or one might be able to rationalize the absence of rights in a particular society or in a segment of that society, for example within a corporation, when overriding sentiments, motivations, rules, and interests work against the realization of those rights for some persons within that system.

The view that rights are universal principles that preempt other considerations is controversial, and the foregoing discussion of needs and interests has scarcely quelled the debate, a debate to which philosophers have been addressing themselves for some time. Those who object to a strong rights thesis might approach the arguments in this book from the following point of view. Given the tentative thesis that every person has equal moral rights, can one equally defend both employee and employer claims to the respect and exercise of rights without harming either party? If this book successfully accomplishes this, then its conclusions should satisfy rights theories and answer the criticisms of proponents of a more utilitarian approach to ethical issues in the workplace.

BASIC MORAL RIGHTS IN THE WORKPLACE

To anticipate the arguments in Parts One and Two, let us briefly see how a theory of basic rights relates to the rights of corporations and employees. Modern business corporations say they have rights to freedom, privacy, and autonomy to conduct business as they wish—very basic rights by the foregoing analysis. So we will have to determine whether and how an *organization* in contrast to a *person* possesses and should be able to exercise such rights. We will have to consider whether the denial of these rights to corporations will harm them, in the sense of taking away their value as productive organizations in a free enterprise economy, in the way that denying human beings these rights harms individuals.

Rights commonly demanded by employees include the rights to due process, to freedom and privacy, to safe working conditions, to fair pay, to participation, and even to a meaningful job. The rights to due process and fair pay, as we shall see in Part Two, are examples of the right to equal consideration. This is because each worker demands objective treatment as an equal in the workplace. The rights to freedom and privacy are derived from the basic right to freedom, which includes autonomy. The right to a safe workplace comes from the right to life, since work hazards threaten the very existence of employees. The rights to participation and to a meaningful job are interpretations of a positive right to freedom since these rights make demands on others to assist workers in their development in the workplace. The issue here is whether or not basic moral rights do or should extend to privately owned places of work so that their applications in the workplace are justifiable and defensible. What is interesting to notice is that corporations and workers are demanding truly basic moral rights. The logic of these demands and how they can be met are the topics of Parts One and Two.

Part 1

The Moral
Status of
Corporations

INTRODUCTION

Moral rights, such as the rights to freedom and autonomy, are ordinarily
ascribed to persons, but these rights may be ascribed to economic institutions as well, in particular to the modern corporation. The contemporary
economist Milton Friedman argues, for example, that economic freedom
and autonomy are rights properly claimed by corporations, and moreover
that these rights are necessary for the development of political rights.[1] The
question arises, how can it be that institutions such as corporations have
rights? How can the language of moral rights, ordinarily applicable to
individuals, be used to talk about the rights and responsibilities of institutions? And indeed, is this a correct analogy? To decide these issues one
must answer the preliminary question of whether rights can aptly and
adequately be ascribed to institutions. This requires an examination of the
ontological character of corporations. This chapter will examine various
theories about the nature of the corporation. In studying these views of the
corporation, I shall argue that these theories tend either to conflate the
corporation with other kinds of phenomena, or to mistake the concept of
social responsibility for moral responsibility. In the next chapter I shall
suggest a collective model of the corporation, a model that should allow a

---

[1]Milton Friedman, *Capitalism and Freedom* (Chicago: University of Chicago Press, 1962),
especially pp. 7–21.

unique account of corporations and make sense of a notion of corporate moral agency. In Chapter Three I shall argue that because corporations are secondary moral agents, they are morally responsible and may be held accountable for their actions. However, because corporations are collectives that are dependent on persons for their existence, continuation, and moral character, corporate moral claims are valid only in the context of the recognition of moral claims of individuals. Corporations and persons have, at best, equal rights, and the rights of persons take precedence over those of corporations.

In this and the chapters to follow I shall sometimes use the term "constituent" to refer to persons who are owners or employees of corporation, that is, stockholders, boards of directors, executives, managers, and other employees. To lump this disparate group under one name is obviously a gross oversimplification of the different relationships that exist between individuals and corporations. But all these persons, in differing ways, contribute to corporate decision-making procedures and to corporate actions so that in some contexts the simplification is useful.

1

The Concept
of a Corporation

THE STRUCTURE OF MODERN BUSINESS CORPORATIONS

A corporation is an association given legal status by a state charter to operate as a single unit with limited liability over an indefinite period of time. A corporation is originally created by a group of individuals for a specific purpose or purposes. Initially the goals and purposes attributed to a newly incorporated business are those of its founders, which are stated in its charter and exemplified in its initial business activity. In the past the charter of a corporation had to state the specific purpose for which the corporation was created, so that any company wishing to expand its business had to amend its charter. Today, however, most charters incorporate a company "for any legitimate business purpose." One may incorporate for a number of reasons, including efficiency of operation, the ability to form capital by selling shares of stock, and because as shareholders of a corporation individuals are not held personally liable for the financial affairs of the organization. Moreover, in our country profitability, or at least not operating at a loss, is also at least an implicit goal of most business corporations, even though it is not usually stated in the charter. Because most corporations are privately owned, no corporation can survive in our economic system without being financially solvent.

In addition, corporations draw up by-laws that govern their internal affairs, in particular the affairs of the board of directors, who represent shareholder interests. The by-laws regulate the structure of the board of directors, for example the number of directors, the number of directors who are also officers of the corporation ("inside directors") as opposed to directors from the "outside," the terms of office, the method of election of the board and their role in corporate governance, the number of officers in the corporation, and other factors affecting the overall governance of the organization.

A corporation is a unique property arrangement, because it is owned by shareholders but usually managed by other persons hired specifically for that task. The corporation is governed by the board of directors who are usually elected in the manner specified in the by-laws. Shareholders ordinarily do not participate in day-to-day decisions except indirectly through the board of directors. Most boards meet only a few times a year. Their input is by and large to the general governance of the corporation. The board, in turn, hires a chief executive officer (CEO), usually called the president, who actually runs the corporation. In most corporations except for the board of directors every person is an employee and reports to at least one other person or group of persons, the CEO reporting to the board. This point will be important when we take up the notion of employee rights in Part Two. If most corporate constituents are employees, then any theory of employee rights must take into account the claims of all of them.

The internal structure of most corporations is hierarchical, as any organization chart will reveal, with a CEO, (president), vice-presidents and other corporate officers, assistant vice-presidents, managers, etc. The actual functions of a corporation, however, may not be linearly hierarchical. In large corporations the hierarchical structure becomes a labyrinth of interrelationships. John Kenneth Galbraith, for example, describes the organization of contemporary American corporations as a series of concentric circles. The officers and the board of directors are in the innermost circle, vice presidents are in the next ring, then managers, and so on, to the parttime temporary unskilled laborers who occupy the outermost ring of the circle.[1] Many successful companies deliberately try to break up or diffuse traditional hierarchical structures either by constantly shifting persons into new positions or by retitling jobs or reallocating responsibilities. In any corporation, however, there are officers and managers to whom others report and whose responsibilities for corporate operations are supposedly greater, and remuneration in most corporations is based, at least in part, on one's title and responsibilities.

In most corporations every job in the company has attached to it certain duties. These job specifications may be merely vague expectations or detailed rules for what counts as minimum or proper job performance.

[1]See John Kenneth Galbraith, *The New Industrial State* (Boston: Houghton Mifflin, 1978).

These job specifications or expectations delineate what counts as a constituent action on behalf of the corporation.

Decision-making within corporations is complex and usually hierarchical. Decisions are made by individuals and committees, and revised by other individuals and committees until the final decision usually little resembles its ancestor. Moreover, decision-making is rule-governed. Certain persons or divisions within a corporation have responsibilities for certain kinds of decisions, others for evaluating them, and still others may reverse or reject decisions. The constituent decision-maker's place in the hierarchical structure and his job description determine the scope and influence of the decisions he or she contributes to the corporation. Moreover, as a constituent, his decisions often take on a formal or anonymous character. One makes decisions "for the corporation" or for the success of some specific project. The choice often becomes impersonal. It is not "my choice" but rather a decision for the benefit of the organization. More will be said about the formal character of decision-making in business in Chapter Two.

This brief description of the structure of most modern corporations is, of course, oversimplified. Every corporation operates differently, and the personalities of its constituents affect the structure as well as the goals of individual corporations. But this outline of the general character of corporate structure will be useful in later chapters when we talk about the nature of corporate action.

THE LEGAL STATUS OF CORPORATIONS

In the law corporations are by and large treated as fictional persons, but unlike ordinary persons they are granted an unlimited "life" when chartered by state license. This means that, for the purposes of some legislation, corporations are treated as if they are single units rather than aggregates or conglomerates. Moreover, the courts in this country have extended to the corporation some constitutional rights guaranteed to individual persons. Legal rights to equal protection, due process, freedom of the press, and freedom from self-incrimination and unreasonable search, are, to some extent, extended to corporations.[2] Recently the Su-

---

[2]See *Bank of the United States* v. *Deveaux,* 9 U.S. (5 Cranch) 61, 86, 91 (1809), where the corporation is defined as a "person" before the courts and thus given equal protection under the law. See also *Santa Clara County* v. *Southern Pacific R.R.,* 118 U.S. 394, 396 (1886). See *Minneapolis & St. L. Ry.* v. *Beckwith,* 129 U.S. 26, 28, 36 (1889), where the corporation is afforded due process under the law. See *Grosjean* v. *American Press Co.,* 297 U.S. 233, 244 (1936), where the corporation is allowed freedom of the press. See *Hale* v. *Henkel,* 201 U.S. 43, 76 (1906), where the corporation is exempt from unreasonable searches and seizures of its property. See Charles R. O'Kelley, Jr., "The Constitutional Rights of Corporations Revisited: Social and Political Expression and the Corporation after *First National Bank* v. *Bellotti,*" *Georgetown Law Review,* 67 (1979), pp. 1347–84, for further analysis of the corporation as a person under the law.

preme Court of the State of Massachusetts extended to the corporation
First Amendment rights to engage in political activities. In a highly controversial decision the Court decided that a corporation could not be prohibited from making contributions or spending money to influence voters so
long as they did not affect the business of the corporation.[3] This decision
adds to the rights afforded to corporations as fictional persons under the
law. Corporations are not full persons under the law, however. For example, the courts have denied corporations the privilege to plead the Fifth
Amendment to avoid self-incrimination, and the courts have denied corporations some of the rights to protection due to persons under the Fourteenth Amendment.[4] Notice, however, that these are all *legal* rights ascribed to a legally fictional person created by incorporation. Whether or
not *moral* rights should be ascribed to corporations will be the topic of
Chapter Three.

The analogy between corporations and persons under the law has
raised the question of whether corporations are sufficiently like individual
human beings that they can be considered to be moral as well as legal
persons and thus have moral rights. The identification of a corporation as a
moral person, however, is a highly questionable thesis. Some theorists have
gone so far as to argue that if the ascription of personhood to corporations
is erroneous, then corporations are merely associations of individuals. The
corporation is not a distinct entity at all, according to this view, so one
cannot ascribe to it rights and responsibilities. Rather, individuals who
work for, manage, or own the corporation have the sole responsibility for
any so-called corporate "actions," and are the proper recipients of "corporate" praise or blame. Sometimes the corporation is compared to an organism or a machine. Still other positions focus on the moral relationships of
corporations to society in terms of a social contract theory or some notion
of social responsibility. In what follows we shall critically examine these
theories.

MORAL PERSONHOOD AND THE CORPORATION

In a recent article, "The Corporation as a Moral Person," Peter French
argues that corporations are "members of the moral community."[5] They,
like their biological counterparts, are moral persons. French points out,
rightly, that one cannot argue that corporations are persons merely because in fact corporations are sometimes treated like persons. Rights and
autonomy under the law are not identical with moral personhood. If future

[3]*First National Bank* v. *Bellotti*, 435 U.S. 765 (1978).
[4]*Northwestern National Life Insurance Co.* v. *Riggs*, 203 U.S. 243, 252, 255 (1906).
[5]Peter French, "The Corporation as a Moral Person," *American Philosophical Quarterly*,
16 (1979), p. 210.

generations develop laws governing the activities of robots, laws similar to the ones governing persons, this will not make robots people.

According to French, a legal person is defined as an eliminatable "subject of a right."[6] Eliminatable subjects, "cannot dispose of their rights, cannot administer them . . . ."[7] From this definition French suggests that a moral person might be defined as a non-eliminatable subject of a right. A non-eliminatable subject is an agent capable of disposing of her rights and administering them, that is, a subject to whom one ascribes moral responsibility. By moral responsibility French has in mind accountability "relationships which hold reciprocally and without prior agreements among moral persons."[8] The sources of moral responsibility, according to French, are the intentional acts of the agent. So in order to be a moral person, that is, an agent who participates in morally accountable relationships for which one is responsible, one must, according to French, be an intentional agent. Thus, French argues, intentionality is a necessary condition for moral agency. When we apply this analysis to corporations, we see that a corporation is a moral person if it is a non-eliminatable subject of a right, if it engages in reciprocal responsibility relationships, and if it is an intentional agent.

French's argument is clear and unobjectionable to this point. But he makes the further claim that intentionality is not merely a necessary condition for moral agency, but that it is also a sufficient condition. Therefore if an entity is an intentional agent, it is a moral agent and thus a moral person.[9] That is, all and only intentional agents are moral persons! French then carefully develops a description of corporate internal decision-making structure (CID) which is hierarchical and rule-bound, and which demonstrates that corporations are, or can be, structured as intentional entities. French concludes that because corporations act intentionally, they are moral persons. I shall call this position Thesis I.

French's argument purporting to show that corporations are moral persons may be attacked on several grounds. It has been suggested that if corporations have the constitution of moral persons they become subject to strange sorts of moral judgments. A merger of two corporations would be, under this view of corporate personhood, cannibalism, the abolishing of a corporate charter would be a form of capital punishment, and so forth.[10] But it should be clear that French is not saying that corporations are like biological persons. Rather he is arguing that corporate intentional struc-

    [6]Ibid.

    [7]Ibid.

    [8]Ibid.

    [9]Ibid. p. 215. French calls corporations non-eliminatable Davidsonian agents.

    [10]Richard Konrad, "Morality and Corporations: Avoiding Schizophrenia," read at the Society for Business Ethics Meetings, American Philosophical Western Division Meetings, Detroit, Michigan, April 25, 1980.

ture is sufficiently like intentionality exhibited in moral persons. French has also been accused of confusing corporate actions with actions of employees on behalf of corporations.[11] But this criticism, too, misses the mark. French is talking about the corporation as a single institutional entity, not merely an aggregate of individuals, because he believes that one may ascribe to the corporation characteristics peculiar to, and distinct from, the collection of individuals who make up the institution.

French has been criticized for more stringent reasons. There is a difference between ascribing goals *to* an organization and determining what are the intentions and goals *of* an organization. While it is possible to discover the goals *to* an institution by asking its employees and observing corporate behavior, it is very difficult if not impossible to specify the intentions *of* an organization apart from the intentions of the individual members of that organization. Corporate rules and procedures (CID), according to this view, specify organizational behavior but seldom define the "intent" of those rules or behavior. Thus the question arises as to whether the concept of intentionality can be appropriately ascribed to corporations at all.[12] But the issue we are considering here is not whether or not corporations act. This will be the challenge of Chapter Two. Rather, the questions are: (1) can corporate actions be said to be intentional actions, and if so, (2) does intentionality always imply moral agency? Finally, (3) even if corporations are intentional agents, are they moral persons?

To understand what is at issue one needs to be clear about the term "intention." An intention may be defined as a deliberate disposition to do something in a certain manner or to realize a state of affairs. An intentional act involves both beliefs and desires and a self-conscious tendency to act in a certain way to realize an outcome based on these beliefs and desires.[13] Intentional actions are ordinarily ascribed to human persons because persons can act upon beliefs and desires and describe their actions in these terms. "I believed he was home, so I went to call on him," "I was hungry, so I made dinner," or "I meant to give you that paper, but I forgot." Intentional language is also often used to describe unstated but implied behavior, as in the statement, "He is waiting at the bus stop, so I assume he will take the bus," or to predict behavior such as the likely moves of one's opponent at chess.

Interestingly, intentional language is useful in describing and predicting the behavior of collectives. For example, Russian troup maneuvers along the Polish border are interpreted to predict the USSR's unstated intentions to invade Poland. One can even use intentional language to

---

[11]John Danley, "Corporate Agency: The Case for Anthropological Bigotry," presented at the Conference on Action and Responsibility, Bowling Green State University, Saturday, May 3, 1980.

[12]Michael Keeley, "Organizations as Non-Persons," *Journal of Value Inquiry*, 15 (1981), pp. 149–55.

[13]See G. E. M. Anscombe, *Intention* (Oxford: Basil Blackwell, 1957), especially p. 11.

describe and predict the actions of complex machines such as computers. For example, a computer can be programmed to play a good game of chess. The computer "learns" to respond to human or other computer opponent moves and often beats even good human chess players. One would not say that the computer *has* intentions in the way one would say that a person has intentions, but in describing the computer's actions one could describe its responsive chess-playing actions with intentional language, for example, "It tried to draw out my Queen."

Because of the various applications of intentional language it is useful to call those phenomena which exhibit intentional behavior, "intentional systems." The contemporary philosopher Daniel Dennett defines an intentional system as "a system whose behavior can be—at least sometimes—explained and predicted by relying on ascriptions to the system of beliefs and desires (and hopes, fears, intentions, hunches . . .)."[14] Dennett says further that this definition of an intentional system does not imply that all so-called intentional systems really have beliefs and desires. Rather, his point is that one can best explain and predict the behavior of a variety of phenomena by describing this behavior in terms of intentional beliefs and desires.[15] Dennett's description of intentional systems is helpful because it shows how taking what he calls an "intentional stance"[16] can accurately describe and predict certain kinds of activities. It helps to predict the computer's chess-playing behavior, it helps to describe human actions, and it is helpful in describing the actions of entities such as corporations. For example, one can use intentional language to describe corporation actions, employing expressions such as, "Did Hooker Chemical Company intend to inflict harm on persons living near Love Canal?," "Did the Ford Motor Company intend to make a dangerous automobile?," "Did the oil companies intend to raise prices?," and so on. From this analysis one could call a corporation an intentional system because one can predict corporate behavior through intentional descriptions. Although one could also describe the same corporate behavior using other modes of description, there is nevertheless "good reason" to describe corporate actions and omissions through the language of intentionality. The good reason, however, is not that a corporation is a moral person, but rather that corporations act as units and exhibit intentional behavior.

It seems obvious that intentionality plays a role in actions for which an agent is to be held morally responsible. One is often held responsible for actions that are within one's capacity to perform. These actions are usually ones one has caused, and may be a result of what was intended by the

---

[14]Daniel Dennett, *Brainstorms* (Montgomery, Vt.: Bradford Books, 1978), p. 33. Copyright © 1978 by The MIT Press, Cambridge, Mass. Excerpt reprinted by permission of The MIT Press and Harvester Press, England.

[15]Ibid., p. 271–75.

[16]Ibid., p. 271.

agent. But even if one grants French's point that all moral agents are intentional agents, and if one brackets the question of whether all moral acts are intentional acts, it does not follow that all intentional systems are moral agents. There are many reasons for this. First, one can construct a computer system that appears to have desires and beliefs in its responses. These computers "act," and computer addicts ascribe to them intentional "beliefs and desires" such as the desire to win when they play chess. But one does not ordinarily ascribe moral agency to these machines. That is, we do not think of computers as non-eliminatable subjects.

To complicate this point let us consider a mythical example. One might imagine a corporation that was operated solely by robots and computers. Such an organization, let us call it Robotron, would have a charter and legal status. It would operate like other corporations. It would own property, manufacture products, conduct marketing, correspond with other corporations and with customers, replace obsolete equipment, develop new product lines, write proxy statements, answer SEC inquiries, etc. Robotron would have stockholders and pay out dividends. It could draw up rules for robot-corporate behavior, and could develop corporate goals and a hierarchy. The rules and structure of its electronic decision-making could be such that one might call Robotron an intentional system.

But is Robotron a moral agent? I think not. This is because Robotron's choices are preprogrammed. For example, it cannot *not* manufacture something that is faulty unless it is programmed not to do so. In simple terms, Robotron cannot "change its 'mind'." Like the chess-playing computer it cannot control what it will choose nor can it refuse to act unless programmed to do so. In French's terms, Robotron cannot administer or dispose of its rights. It is neither free nor autonomous. And just as one cannot hold a computer responsible for its defeats in chess, so too, one cannot hold Robotron responsible for poor products or faulty service. Because Robotron can neither choose nor choose *not* to choose, it cannot respond to the moral intentions of others, and it is incapable of moral action.

This illustration is helpful in showing how something like a robot or a computer can be constructed to exhibit complex intentional behavior without being a moral agent. French, however, would object to these examples as showing merely that one could in fact construct an intentional system that, biologically, was not a person. But this system is constructed by other intentional agents, that is, by persons. That a system such as Robotron exhibits intentional behavior, then, is not surprising. What French means, or should mean, is that nonhuman intentional systems constructed by humans can display intentional behavior that *appears* to exhibit moral agency. However, one would not want to ascribe moral agency, and thus moral responsibility, to computers or to Robotron because neither of these intentional systems is capable of administrating and disposing of its own "rights." Further, neither can be held morally accountable or reciprocally responsible for the moral intentions of others. Neither can meet any of French's criteria for a non-eliminatable subject. Thus one must distinguish between intentional systems that display intentional behavior but are not intentional agents, and intentional systems such as persons who both display intentional behavior and *are* intentional agents.

Even if not all intentional systems are moral agents, French's argument might hold in the more restricted case of intentional systems that are made up of, and run by, individual persons, namely intentional systems such as corporations or countries. And indeed French's argument is directed to these sorts of systems. The more restricted and more relevant question is, then, are humanly constituted intentional systems such as corporations moral persons? Are corporations non-eliminatable subjects?

Now it is tempting to think that corporations are non-eliminatable subjects because many corporations appear to think about their desires, beliefs and goals, and some corporations or persons acting on behalf of corporations seem to engage in moral self-analysis as well. For example, during the Vietnamese War the Dow Chemical Company claimed to have debated about the morality of manufacturing napalm, the defoliant used in Vietnam.[17] The problem with examples such as this one is that it is not corporations who engage in self-reflection and moral self-analysis, but rather their *constituents* who do so on behalf of the corporation. In the case of Dow, its board of directors debated the morality of manufacturing napalm. Dow's so-called "actions" were a result of the actions of persons who functioned as agents for the corporation. To continue the example, Dow *was* responsible for the manufacture of napalm. But the corporation in fact did not manufacture napalm; persons working for the corporation did so. We hold Dow responsible because the persons who made napalm were acting as agents on behalf of the corporation. We then say that the corporation performs intentional actions. But literally the actions are a result of the activities of a collection of persons or groups operating as a single unit. Thus the intricate web of intentional behavior exhibited in the CID coupled with resulting actions by agents on behalf of the corporation produce what appear to be corporate "actions."

The result is that corporations exhibit intentional behavior and are said to act. But both their so-called intentions and their "actions" are the collective result of decisions made by individual persons. The corporation is an eliminatable subject because without persons, corporate "actions" literally could not occur.

The problems with French's analysis are that he tries to equate intentionality with moral agency, identifies moral agency with moral person-

---

[17]See Earl A. Molander, "Product Stewardship at Dow Chemical Company." *Responsive Capitalism* (New York: McGraw Hill Book Company, 1980), pp. 38–50.

hood, and conflates the notion of a corporation with that of an individual person. French might rejoin that he was merely pointing out the features of intentionality evident in corporations, and this is a promising feature of his analysis. But his appeal to moral personhood to describe the structure of corporations detracts from an examination of the unique features of corporations as institutions rather than as persons.

Finally, French's analysis raises a difficult question from an ethical perspective. If a corporation is a moral person, what is the status of employee-persons? Are they lesser moral persons? An employee, by this reasoning, could be a moral person of grade one, MP^1, a corporate committee making decisions a MP^2, etc., so that a corporation would be an MP^n. A corporation would be allowed to do as it pleases so long as it did not interfere with the freedoms of other corporations (other MP^ns). But by this reasoning, a corporation could interfere with the freedoms of MP^1s without violating them, because, being MP^ns, corporations would have more *moral freedom* than persons or MP^1s. French's analysis may give so much to corporations in the way of moral personhood that individuals end up having less moral status than corporations.[18]

CORPORATIONS AS ASSOCIATIONS

In contrast to the definition of a corporation as a moral person, a second view of corporations picks up on French's suggestion that moral agency and moral personhood are synonymous, but this position rejects his claim that the corporation itself is a moral person. Rather, it states that

> a corporation is in fact an association of individuals who are entitled to the same rights and legal protections which apply to all other individuals and organizations.[19]

According to this thesis a corporation is not a distinct entity having its own personality, intentions, rights, and liabilities. A corporation is rather an aggregate of individuals who voluntarily get together for the purposes of convenience, efficiency, and limited liability to conduct a business. The term "corporation" is merely a mental construct or convention used to describe the particular legal contractual relationship represented by the voluntary association.[20] Let us call this position Thesis II.

Thesis II develops the aggregate concept of a corporation from the

---

[18]See Michael Keeley, "Organizations as Non-Persons," *Journal of Value Inquiry,* 15 (1981), pp. 149–55.

[19]Robert Hesson, *In Defense of the Corporation* (Stanford: Hoover Institution Press, 1979), p. xv. Excerpts reprinted by permission of the Hoover Institution Press.

[20]Ibid., pp. 41–42, and Roger Pilon, "Corporations and Rights: On Treating Corporate People Justly," *Georgia Law Review,* 13 (1979), pp. 1245–1370.

following sorts of considerations. Individual persons create institutions such as corporations through voluntary associations that develop economic relationships. These relationships are legally formalized by contract, a contract which refers to the association as a *corporation*. However, "*Every* organization, regardless of its legal form or features, consists only of individuals."[21] The corporation consists only of persons; there is nothing—no entity—distinct from the owners, managers, and employees of the association.

According to this theory the actions of individuals within a corporation and through its board of directors cause corporate "action." A board of directors is representative of shareholder interests. It can change the direction, scope, or size of an organization, or even shut it down. But a corporation itself does not act at all because it is not a "something." Everything that occurs in and through the corporation is a result of individual decision-making, individual action or omission. Therefore, according to this analysis, all so-called corporate "actions" can be traced ultimately to individuals, each of whom in different ways plays an important role in shaping the direction of the association or aggregate. And the corporation is merely the sum of these individual actions and of the complex interactions between them. Notice that the aggregate theory of the corporation almost neglects the fact that corporations as units have legal status because of their state license and the status conferred to them by the courts.

The implication of this thesis for an evaluation of corporate moral agency is the following. If a corporation is an association of individuals, then when the association "acts," moral responsibility needs to be traced back to the individual or individuals making the decision. Thus "anyone who proposes to deny or destroy the rights of a corporation is really attacking individual rights."[22] Similarly, those questioning corporate moral agency are really questioning the moral agency of persons who comprise the corporation. Therefore, any description of corporate moral agency, moral responsibility, or institutional rights simply restates the individual responsibilities and rights of corporate constituents.

Thesis II, which is defended by a number of contemporary economists, is interesting because it identifies any so-called "corporate moral agency" with the sum of the individual moral views of its constituents and thereby avoids some of the philosophical difficulties inherent in describing a corporation as a unit like a moral person. The latter position is always problematic because, to put it simply, it is difficult to identify the invisible entity called "The Corporation" apart from its employees, stockholders, buildings, land, etc. This difficulty will be discussed in the next chapter. However, the problem with Thesis II is that it is an incomplete account of

[21]Hesson, p. 41.
[22]Hesson, p. 46.

the corporation. It erroneously identifies the causal role of the individual in corporate decision-making with the outcome of that process: corporate "action." Let me elaborate.

Even if there are no perceivable entities around called "Corporations," this does not mean that one cannot make sense out of describing the corporation as some sort of unit. We often praise or blame corporations even when it is virtually impossible to trace their actions to individuals. For example, Hooker Chemical Company has been accused of polluting the Love Canal in upstate New York. Who is responsible? Is it the person or persons who actually dumped chemicals into the Love Canal? Is it the managers who knew about and directed the action? Is it the chemists at Hooker who knew or did not know about the dangers of the chemicals and did or did not inform executives at Hooker? Most of these persons are unknown; many who are known have left the company. Yet we attribute at least some of the responsibility and blame to the company itself.[23] In the next chapters more will be said about the nature of corporate moral agency and moral responsibility. What is important here is to see how it is that we can talk about corporations as if they were distinct entities, not mere aggregates. The aggregate theory may be correct, but if so, it must account for both the legal and ordinary ways in which we refer to corporations.

CORPORATIONS AS MACHINES

If the notion of personhood does not fit the descriptions of a corporation and if corporations are not mere aggregates, then it is sometimes argued that corporations are formal organizations directed to economic ends. Let us call this proposal Thesis III. A machine analogy is useful to describe corporate organizational structure, according to this thesis. Corporations are organized like machines or are enough like machines such as Robotron that they, like Robotron, cannot be ascribed any rights whatsoever. According to John Ladd, corporate rules and operating procedures, like the design and structure of a machine, are set up to achieve external economic ends rather than designed in relation to, or as a consequence of, member employees.[24] Each employee in a corporation, like each part in a machine, plays an important role in achieving corporate ends.

> A distinctive mark of such organizations is that they make a clear-cut distinction between the acts and relationships of individuals in their official capacity within the organization and in their private capacity. Decisions of individual

---

[23]See Michael Brown, "Love Canal and the Poisoning of America," *Atlantic*, Fall 1979, pp. 33–47.

[24]John Ladd, "Morality and the Ideal of Rationality in Formal Organizations," *Monist*, 54 (1970), pp. 488–516.

decision-makers in the organization are attributed to the organization and not to the individual. In that sense, they are impersonal.[25]

In the corporate structure any weak or dissident employee, like any malfunctioning part, could be, and should be, replaced in order for the whole to operate at maximum corporate efficiency. Therefore, while corporate activities are rule-governed, these rules, as impersonal operating procedures, preclude rather than imply moral agency. And just as it is silly to ascribe moral responsibilities to machines, so too, the organization, structure, and goals of a corporation suggest that it does not make sense to ascribe to it moral responsibilities.[26]

The consequences of a view such as Ladd's are best illustrated by reexamining the computer corporation Robotron. Suppose Robotron began manufacturing toxic substances injurious to the health of anyone who came in contact with the substances. Societal mechanisms would interfere with Robotron's program and alter its manufacturing techniques to prohibit further manufacture of these toxic substances. No one would accuse Robotron of moral irresponsibility; it just happened to manufacture socially unacceptable substances. Nor would we accuse society of interfering with the rights and freedoms of Robotron since, as a formal organization made up of nonhumans, Robotron *has* no rights or freedoms. According to Thesis III any formal organization that operates impersonally could be, in principle, in the same position as Robotron. Because it neither understands the concept of moral responsibility nor acts as a moral agent, such an institution has no rights, and it cannot expect to be treated as a free autonomous agent. Society, moreover, should feel no moral compunction in enforcing its demands on such an institution.[27]

The machine analogy is useful in accounting for corporate behavior in cases where corporations appear not to be aware that they have moral as well as economic responsibilities. If corporations are formal organizations, then moral considerations are not taken into account except when they are important for economic ends. The difficulty with the machine analogy is that it cannot account for the nonmechanistic behavior in which many corporations engage. For example, in the recent controversy involving the dangers of tampons Proctor and Gamble, the manufacturer of Rely tampon, withdrew its product from the market within 24 hours after it was suggested that Rely tampon might cause the fatal disease, toxic shock syndrome. This action was taken by Proctor and Gamble without legal pressure from the government and before there was any public moral outcry.[28]

[25]Ibid., p. 488.

[26]Ibid., pp. 488–516; Patricia H. Werhane, "Formal Organizations, Economic Freedom and Moral Agency," *Journal of Value Inquiry,* 14 (1980), pp. 43–50.

[27]See Werhane, "Formal Organizations," p. 44 for the Robotron example.

[28]*Chicago Tribune,* May 4, 1981, p. 88.

The difference between Robotron and Proctor and Gamble is that Proctor and Gamble is managed by human beings who, unlike Robotron, do not always act in predictable ways and do not always follow their job-prescribed role responsibilities. Moral and immoral issues sometimes enter into the decision-making process of the corporations, even in corporations that try to operate strictly as formal organizations. Moral issues enter into corporate decision-making in another way, too. Because corporations, unlike Robotron, exist in a social and political context, it is impossible to ignore all social pressures. Robotron, for example, would not have responded to the tampon scare unless it was programmed to do so or required to do so by law. But corporations operated by human persons often *do* respond. The machine analogy cannot account for this sort of response.[29]

Thesis III ends philosophical dialogue. It supposes that no sense can be made of the corporation except as a formal organization incapable of moral response. This thesis is of interest primarily because it is simple, in fact so simple that it is unacceptable as a complete description of a corporation. It cannot account for the strange ways in which corporations do react to socio-cultural moral demands. Notice that this view is similar to French's in the sense that both theories denigrate the role of the employee in the corporation. Such views are antithetical to the claim that individuals are autonomous and have certain rights, rights that preempt organizational concerns. In Chapter Two I shall claim that even if the employee appears to be relegated to a secondary role this need not be the case, given the proper analysis of the corporation.

CORPORATIONS, ORGANISMS AND SOCIAL RESPONSIBILITY

Another sort of thesis that tries to ascribe some sort of moral agency to corporations argues, in brief, that the notion of corporate responsibility should be explained in terms of social responsibility. As part of a social order corporations have certain kinds of responsibilities to the society in which they operate. It is then claimed that we can ascribe such responsibilities to corporations, and that such responsibility can be defined as "moral accountability." We shall call this set of arguments Thesis IV.[30]

To make this sort of argument the philosopher Kenneth Goodpaster

---

[29]See Kenneth Goodpaster, "Morality and Organizations," in *Ethical Issues in Business,* 2nd ed., Thomas Donaldson and Patricia H. Werhane, eds. (Englewood Cliffs, N.J.: Prentice-Hall, Inc., 1982), pp. 137–44.

[30]Both Kenneth Goodpaster and Thomas Donaldson appear to argue this way in certain articles. Kenneth Goodpaster, ibid., pp. 137–144. Thomas Donaldson, "Moral Change and the Corporation," *Proceedings of the Bentley College Second National Conference on Business Ethics,* W. Michael Hoffman, ed. (Washington, D.C.: University Press of America, 1979), pp. 83–90. See also Kenneth Goodpaster's article in the same volume.

claims that corporations operate somewhat like organisms. Corporations, like other organisms, interact with society through various feedback mechanisms. Just as the environment and societal expectations trigger certain kinds of responses in other organisms, so too, corporations often act or react according to the kinds of feedback they receive from society. If this model accurately describes corporations, then, it is argued, a "space" exists in which a corporation might be expected to adopt moral goals in response to community criticism or esteem.

The idea that corporations can adopt moral goals is further developed. Even in the pursuit of economic ends corporations often react to moral restraints imposed on them by society. Moreover, it is not impossible, and indeed it is highly plausible, to suggest corporations that could and in fact do adopt moral goals. These goals could be institutionalized within the corporation in such a way that they would become ends for which a corporation operates. For example, a corporation could adopt a policy of hiring qualified minorities without giving up its goal of economic gain.

This kind of argument enhances the concept of what a corporation is by showing that it is not impossible for a corporation to adopt goals that we would ordinarily label "moral". I would suggest, however, that Thesis IV has not succeeded in demonstrating that corporations are moral entities, because other organisms such as domestic animals, which are not moral agents, also respond to social (moral) pressures. Moreover, the fact that particular corporations have adopted moral goals in response to societal feedback or have institutionalized morally appropriate behavior as a corporate aim means that such corporations could be labeled "socially responsible." But social responsibility is different from, and does not necessarily entail, moral responsibility.

This point needs elaboration. What I am suggesting is that the qualitative value of institutional goals does not necessarily determine whether or not the institution is a moral agent. CARE has highly commendable goals, and most of its employees are not robots. But CARE could be run by Robotron. If it is the case that a corporation such as Robotron can operate as a socially responsible organization, it is obvious that merely to alter the goals of a corporation does not, in itself, alter the character of the institution. Therefore one may assign corporation goals that are morally commendable and that may be instituted as part of corporate operating procedures. Corporations with such goals are socially responsible institutions and deserve society's commendation, but even they are not necessarily moral agents. This is because social responsibility does not necessarily imply moral agency. To ascribe to corporations social responsibility without ascribing to them moral responsibility might be enough to elicit acceptable behavior from them, but philosophers who hold Thesis IV also imply that corporations *are* moral agents. This, however, does not follow from the theory.

THE SOCIAL CONTRACT THEORY

The social contract theory focuses primarily not on how corporations are constituted, but instead on their status in society. According to this position, in brief, because a corporation is sanctioned by society to operate in a given community, the corporation makes some implicit commitments to that community. These commitments form the basis for the social contract between corporations and society. A corporation is allowed to exist because it is thought that

> the benefits from authorizing the existence of productive organizations outweigh the detriments of doing so. . . . From the standpoint of society, the goal of a productive organization may be said to be *to enhance the welfare of society through a satisfaction of consumer and worker interests.*[31]

Society has high expectations for corporations, and because they are allowed to exist and operate freely, corporations have obligations to achieve these expectations. A corporation that does not live up to its side of the bargain is not performing its obligations within the community, and thus is not upholding its contract.

The social contract theory is a major contribution to the analysis of modern business corporations. Its emphasis on the obligations of corporations provides an important insight into the scope of corporate moral responsibility, an issue which had not been previously explored. The theory assumes that corporations are moral agents, but it is less clear as to what this agency entails. This theory needs to be supplemented with a definitive analysis of the ontological nature of the corporation in order to account fully for the nature of corporate societal responsibility. Moreover, while the theory focuses on external corporate-societal relationships, this book takes a narrower look at corporations in terms of their internal structure and their relationships to employees. Neither point of view can be ignored if one is to have a clear notion of the corporation and its moral behavior.

CORPORATIONS AND THE LAW

Let us consider the following suggestion. It may or may not be philosophically valid to speak of corporate moral agency. There are difficulties with the identity of a corporation as an aggregate or as a collective. One could decide that the metaphysical question of corporate moral agency, while interesting for philosophical discourse, if of little practical consequence. The problem of greater concern is whether or not corporations can be

---

[31]Thomas Donaldson, *Corporations and Morality* (Englewood Cliffs, N.J.: Prentice-Hall, Inc., 1982), pp. 44–49.

influenced to respond to societal moral demands. If corporations respond to societal feedback and "behave themselves" morally, the theoretical question of whether or not corporations are persons or moral agents is of little relevance. Let us call this position Thesis VI.[32]

According to Thesis VI, instead of expending philosophical energy in a metaphysical analysis of the corporation, one should create legal *sanctions* against corporate behavior society dislikes or, better yet, one should create legal *incentives* to societally acceptable corporate behavior. Such incentives and sanctions would make more sense to corporations than praise or blame. Moreover, they could be internalized so as to affect the cost of doing business and consequently would be more effective than regulations that impose force from outside. Such incentives and sanctions would make what society thinks are immoral actions so costly that it would be more prudent for a corporation to be moral. The legal expert Christopher Stone suggests a complicated system of enterprise liabilities wherein a corporation would bear the costs of societally abhorrent injuries, such as consumer damages, pollution, misuse of scarce natural resources, and the like. Which injuries would be those for which a corporation is liable would be determined by society, and the liability included in the cost of doing business.[33]

Similarly, the economist Charles Schultze proposes that market incentives such as tax incentives or transfer payments be used rather than regulation to control corporate behavior. For example, tax incentives could be given to corporations that provide safe working conditions for their employees and this should be coupled with what Schultze calls an "injury-rate tax" paid for every employee hurt at his or her job. In this manner, Schultze argues, one would be using market incentives, which corporations understand, to regulate their behavior.[34]

These and other suggestions for corporate reform present no problems for the practical philosopher. But even if legal sanctions and incentives do produce appropriate corporate performance, we must give an adequate account of the ontological nature of the corporation before we can talk about the internal affairs of corporations and to make sense out of the relationships of employees to the organization.

CONCLUSION

Six views of the corporation have been presented, each of which attempts to account for the nature of a corporation. Each of these accounts is inade-

[32]Christopher Stone hinted at this sort of position at the Notre Dame Conference on "Conscience and the Corporation," February 1980.

[33]Christopher Stone, "The Place of Enterprise Liability in the Control of Corporate Conduct," *Yale Law Journal*, 90 (1980), pp. 1–75.

[34]Charles Schultze, *The Public Use of Private Interest* (Washington, D.C.: The Brookings Institution, 1977).

quate but each, for different reasons adds to an understanding of a corporation. By drawing attention to corporate intentionality, the moral person theory shows how it is that corporations at least appear to act as intentional systems. The aggregate theory points out the important role of constituents in corporate activities. The machine theory reveals how corporations and their constituents can adopt disinterested moral atitudes, and the organism theory points to the limits of that disinterestedness in corporate action. The social contract theory emphasizes the moral relationship between corporations and society, a relationship further explored in examining corporations and the law. However, none of these theories answers the question what is unique to the character of corporations. This will be the task of the next chapter.

2

Corporations and Institutional Moral Agency

A clear-cut concept of the corporation is essential for the analysis of responsibilities in business, and to ascertain whether or not corporations truly have, or should be ascribed, moral rights to freedom and autonomy as Milton Friedman suggests. In order to say that corporations have moral rights and thus can justifiably exercise them, one must make the prior claim that corporations are moral agents. In order to determine whether or not corporations are moral agents, in Chapter One we considered the views of various philosophers, who have depicted the corporation as an organism and even as a moral person—an entity ethically identical to a human person. Other philosophers have precluded the assignment of moral agency to corporations by describing them as associations of individuals or as machines. Such explanations serve as partial descriptions of the corporation, but each compares the corporation to another phenomenon and thereby fails to discover what features are unique to these institutions. Consequently each of these depictions for different reasons sheds inadequate light on whether or not corporations are, in any sense, moral agents, and thus might have claims to moral rights.

In this chapter some of the elements of each of these formulas will be used to describe the corporation. A corporation is neither identical to an individual moral person nor is it an association devoid of moral responsibility as a unit. Rather, the theory I shall propose will combine elements of two principles called respectively, ontological individualism and meth-

odological collectivism. Corporations are made up of individuals. Ontologically they have no special identity over and above the individuals who
constitute them. Unlike aggregates, corporations can be said in a peculiar
sense to "act," but unlike persons, all corporate actions are secondary actions that result from a series of primary actions by persons. Corporations
function, then, as if they were real, autonomous, individual entities. Because
of this, an aggregate theory of the corporation is inadequate as either an
explanation of how corporations act or of how individuals act on behalf of a
corporation. Thus, I shall argue, corporations are what I shall call *secondary
collectives*, whose actions are ontologically reducible to, but not identical
with, actions of individuals performing on behalf of the corporation. This
depiction of corporate collective action will ascribe to corporations sufficient secondary or institutional moral agency to justify the ascription of a
form of moral responsibility as well.

ONTOLOGICAL INDIVIDUALISM AND CORPORATIONS

Corporations are strange sorts of constructions. They are no more than
their constituents, and yet a corporation often functions as a collective. In
this section I shall show why it is that corporations are not ontologically real
individuals. In the next sections I shall discuss their functional collective
nature.

A corporation is not an independent entity. Corporations are constituted by, and exist and function only because of, their constituents. In
ordinary parlance we often speak of the actions of corporations. Corporations sue each other, they manufacture, sell and recall goods, and other
services. Corporations buy and sell property and stocks, they have bank
accounts. Corporations hire and fire workers, they employ lawyers and
accountants and advertising agencies. These and many other kinds of actions are actions we attribute to a corporation as if it were an autonomous
individual. But there are some peculiarities about corporate actions. No
one ever "sees" a corporation, per se. A corporation does not appear in
court, it does not shake hands or speak on television. A corporation is not
that sort of phenomenon. It is a sort of fiction that is represented by
constituents and outside agents who do these sorts of jobs. Boards of directors, stockholders, and management make decisions for the corporation.
Other persons carry out these decisions in making and selling products.
Still other persons—outside agents such as lawyers, accountants, advertising agencies, and public relations persons—are hired by the corporation to
carry out other activities on its behalf. So-called corporate actions are,
therefore, results of certain actions of these individuals acting to achieve a
certain corporate goal. Even Robotron was created by individual persons
and could be shut down by their actions. Therefore the "actions" of a

corporation are not literally actions of a physical entity, but rather, "actions" that are represented and carried out through persons. Consequently, no corporation can be said to "act on its own." Corporations have no reality over and above their constituents, because they are created by and function only because of them. Thus corporations cannot exist independently of their constituency in any ontologically independent way.[1]

METHODOLOGICAL COLLECTIVISM AND CORPORATIONS

To argue that corporations are not real, independent individuals does not automatically eliminate the possibility of collective corporate action. Because the "actions" of corporations depend on the actions of constituents and outside agents, without which there would be no corporate activity, it is tempting to say that all so-called "actions" of the corporation may simply be redescribed as actions of the individuals who initiate the activity. Indeed, this is the position of those who hold an aggregate theory of the corporation. But, this overstates the case. For example, one could, with a great deal of effort, trace the original designers of the Pinto automobile, the persons who approved the design and decided to manufacture the Pinto, the thousands of workers who made and sold the auto, the persons who knew of its design difficulties, and the individuals who decided it was cheaper to settle liability suits than to redesign the gas tank. The task of tracing these persons and allocating the proper degrees of praise and blame would be formidable but not altogether impossible. According to the aggregate theory of the corporation this process would result in the appropriate allocation of moral responsibility, and the only reason such a project is not undertaken is that it is too time-consuming and the persons originally responsible for the Pinto are in all likelihood no longer at Ford. I would argue, however, that there is a more important reason why we do not try to reduce all of the actions of a corporation to the actions of individuals who work for or own that organization. This is because we cannot. We cannot because *not all actions of corporations are redescribable merely as individual actions.* There is such a phenomenon as collective corporate action even though the actors are themselves all individuals who contribute to the collective activity. Let us illustrate how this can happen.

For many years, almost from its inception, American Telephone and Telegraph Company (AT&T) prided itself on hiring women and minorities. Recently, however, the government accused AT&T of discrimination because it does not promote women and minorities to management positions.[2] Whether or not this was a deliberate AT&T policy will never be fully

---

[1]See Anthony Quinton, "Social Objects," *Proceedings of the Aristotelian Society*, 76 (1976), pp. 1–27.

[2]Earl A. Molander, "Affirmative Action at AT&T," in Molander, *Responsive Capitalism* (New York: McGraw-Hill Book Company, 1980), pp. 56–70.

determined. As at every company there surely were, and are, persons at AT&T who practice discrimination, but it could be the case that no one person or group of persons ever deliberately discriminated against a woman or a minority. In fact there were no written policies prohibiting the promotion to management positions of these classes of persons. But looking at the pattern of company behavior, it is clear that women and minorities were not promoted. Thus it could be that the "action" attributed to AT&T, "action" which apparently is the sum of a series of individual actions, was discriminatory without there being any specific instance of discrimination that one can pinpoint.

This illustration suggests that in fact not all "actions" of corporations can be analyzed in terms of the actions of individuals who operate on behalf of the corporation. Moreover, corporations often receive praise or blame or are held responsible even when those persons who performed the actions that comprised the corporate activity cannot themselves be held morally liable. But could it not be that the actions of human agents, when certain legal conventions obtain, are merely redescribed as corporate actions? According to this view, in the AT&T case, for example, it is a convenient legal convention to attribute the "actions" to AT&T as if it were an individual agent, even though in fact one could re-analyze all the "actions" of AT&T in terms of actions of constituents and agents working there.

I want to argue, on the contrary, that a re-analysis of what happened at AT&T in terms of constituent and agent actions will not yield the proper explanation of the behavior in question in every case. Or, to put what I want to argue differently, the analysis of discrimination at AT&T in terms of individual actions will uncover the *causes* and *necessary conditions* of that "action," but not the *reasons* for it. In order to show that this is the case, we must develop a theory of secondary collective action that accounts for the differences between aggregate and secondary collective activity.

A THEORY OF SECONDARY ACTION

Let us call the actions of individuals primary actions. Any action of an individual corporate constituent or an outside agent working for the corporation could be a primary action, but it should be noticed that not all actions, even actions of individuals, are primary actions. Often individuals employ other persons to act on their behalf. I recently used a real estate broker to rent my house for the summer. Now I was the rentor of the house, but I did not perform the actions necessary to do this. My action was what some philosophers call a "secondary action."[3] The rental was at-

---

[3]David Copp, "Collective Actions and Secondary Actions," *American Philosophical Quarterly*, 16 (1979), pp. 177–79.

tributed to me, and I would be to blame if things went wrong, but I did not perform the basic actions necessary to rent the house. The contemporary philosopher David Copp states the point this way:

> An agent's action is a secondary action if, and only if, it is correctly attributable to this agent on the basis of either an action of some other agent, or actions of some other agents.[4]

Notice that even if I hire the real estate broker as my agent this does not absolve her of *all* moral responsibility in regard to the rental. The broker is responsible for duties expected of brokers—role duties. If for example it turns out that my renter is some sort of house wrecker, I will hold the broker as well as myself morally blameworthy for not examining his background. What is interesting about the relationship between the broker and myself is that the broker's actions were both *necessary* for the rental to occur since I had no time to rent the house myself, and also *sufficient* for this particular house rental to occur as I would not have rented the house to whom I did without that action. But that action did not absolutely determine my rental because the broker did not force me to sign the lease, and I was free to rent the house to someone else.[5] Further, only actions of the broker without which I could not rent the house count as actions contributing to the secondary action. The fact that the broker kissed her secretary has nothing to do with the rental unless, of course, she interrupted the typing of the lease. More generally, what this example shows in an informal way is that one can accomplish some task without literally doing anything by using agents whose performance of relevant primary actions produces the desired secondary result.

Applying this analysis to corporations, one can see that it makes sense to talk about corporate "action" only if whatever activity is attributed to a corporation is a result of primary actions of individuals. Corporate "actions," then, are secondary actions produced by a series of primary individual actions. Moreover, these primary actions contribute to corporate activity *only* if they are necessary for the corporate activity to take place. For example, some person or persons had to design and invent the Pinto in order for it to be manufactured. But only those actions of the inventor or inventors that contributed to the production of the Pinto count as relevant primary actions. Further, these actions have to be sufficient to result in a secondary action. In the case of the manufacture of the Pinto there must be a series of related primary actions of inventors, manufacturers, and workers, actions without which there would be no automobile. When one says, "Ford produced the Pinto," one is referring, in the first instance, to a collection of primary actions. So if one is to make sense out of corporate

[4]Ibid., p. 177.
[5]Ibid.

"actions" at all, these must be secondary actions. In general, if collectives can be said to "act," their "actions" must necessarily be secondary actions of the sort just described.

However, there is something amiss in the description of corporate actions as secondary actions. In the example of the realtor who acted as my agent, the realtor was authorized by me to act, that is, to rent my house. But if corporations are not individuals and cannot act autonomously, how can they be said to authorize primary actions, authorization which is necessary for the actions to occur? The analogy between individual primary and secondary actions and collective action, then, is imperfect. Corporate secondary action is much more complex than individual secondary action.

COLLECTIVE SECONDARY ACTION

The structure and operations of corporations allow the phenomenon of collective secondary action even though there is no individual authorizer, The Corporation, to initiate the requisite primary actions. Let us see why this is so. The charter and the founders of a corporation set the initial corporate goals and initiate the business of the organization as a corporation. The charter and by-laws specify the goals and the authorization process through which constituents operate. In the complex decision-making processes that occur within a corporation, corporate goals change, and a corporate "personality" or "character" develops. This is due in part to the way in which the original charter is interpreted by corporate constituents, in part to directives of the board of directors and management, and in part to the pressures in the marketplace. Corporate constituents function in terms of these goals, acting in accordance with their interpretation of the directives of the charter or later interpretations of the charter. Even if the goals and directives are vague and impersonal, constituent and agent corporate actions are goal-directed. In acting on behalf of the corporation, constituents, like my realtor, perform primary actions on behalf of the impersonal goals of the corporation. The goals are impersonal because (a) they are anonymously stated in the charter, and/or because (b) they have been radically altered by the board of directors, managers, committees and the market so that they take on an impersonal or anonymous character no longer traceable to individual authors. The difference between actions of my realtor and the actions of corporate constituents is that in the former instance the actor (the realtor) was performing for an individual (me). In the latter the constituent or agent may act on behalf of a nonhuman charter or goal or in compliance with the norms or character of the business. In the first case the realtor and I are responsible for actions done on my behalf. But in at least some instances of corporate action, the constituent or agent is literally acting for a nonhuman "agent."

Related to the foregoing is the consideration that in all except very small corporations constituent actions are often anonymous, that is, they are actions performed "for the corporation" or with the goals of the corporation in mind rather than for personal satisfaction. Corporate decisions are by and large made by committees, and these decisions are reviewed and revised by other persons or other committees. Corporate action is often a result of the functions of disparate groups within a corporation so that an action of one part of a corporation is a function in part, of actions of another group within an organization. An individual action is often unrecognizable when the final "action" is taken or a policy is formulated. For example, the personnel office at AT&T that hires women and minorities could be an exemplary department, hiring only the most qualified persons. Yet some unstated policies at AT&T implemented by managers there disallowed the promotion of women and minorities. The consequent discrimination at AT&T was caused by thousands of primary actions, whose peculiar character was a result of the ways in which the impersonal goals of AT&T were interpreted through particular primary actions.

The final activity or policy, evolving from combinations and permutations of individual primary actions done on the behalf of impersonal aims, is not identified merely with the sum of the original individual tasks. This is because of the anonymity of the individual actions, the ways in which each is changed through the actions of other individuals and groups in other divisions of the corporation, and the ways in which goals are interpreted at each stage of activity. Thus the *reasons* for the corporate "action" in these cases cannot be explained merely by itemizing individual constituent actions.

Thus a corporate "activity" or policy is a secondary action, an action ascribed to the collective, even though the collective itself did not literally authorize the action. This is because the corporate "action" is authorized by the charter, the goals, and the directives interpreted as "corporate directives." These documents or aims themselves undergo a continuous process of depersonalization through interpretation and alteration by various corporate constituents and by the marketplace. Thus collective secondary action is not identical to individual secondary action because of the impersonal character of the authorization process. But the distinction between primary and secondary action is useful in understanding how constituents act impersonally for collectives, and the distinction explains how what we often call corporate "action" is secondary action.

NONDISTRIBUTIVE CORPORATE "ACTION"

The notion of collective secondary action is helpful in understanding why one often holds a corporation and not its constituents and agents primarily responsible for its "actions" even though these actions are secondary actions that a corporation is unable to perform "by itself." This is because a secondary action of a corporation is truly a collective action. Since it is authorized by an impersonal "authority" and carried out formally or disinterestedly by constituents working for the impersonal authority, not every secondary action can be reattributed in every instance to the persons who caused that action to occur. While individual action is necessary for secondary action, and while the totality of individual actions on behalf of a corporation is sufficient for such action, except in the smallest corporations no one individual action is sufficient for a secondary action, and each individual input becomes transformed as it mixes with other constituent and agent input and as corporate "directives" are interpreted. The result is often (but not always) collective action different from the primary actions of its constituents. Thus, at least in principle, it is possible that there could be corporate immoral "action" that is the result of a series of blameless primary actions. For all of these reasons, then, corporate "action" is collective secondary action the rationale for which cannot be redescribed in terms of the actions of constituents, even though these are nevertheless necessary and sufficient for a corporation to function.

Is all corporate "action" of this sort? Probably not. There are surely some "actions" every corporation performs that can be directly traced to an individual or individuals within the corporation. This is especially true when a corporation is very small or is run by a strong or dictatorial president. Thus although the aggregate theory of the corporation is correct as an ontological description of the construction of a corporation, and is useful in explaining many corporate activities, it is inadequate to account for how it is that corporations can "act" in ways that depend on individual actions within the corporation but are not attributable to them.

CORPORATIONS AS INTENTIONAL SYSTEMS

The description of institutional collective "action" is useful in understanding corporate intentionality. A corporation is an intentional system, that is, it exhibits intentional behavior, just as Peter French has suggested. But when one talks about collective intentionality one is not saying that a corporation or a nation thinks, desires, believes, or literally *has* intentions, as French's position implies. There is no psychophysical entity to have such intentions. Rather, a corporate intentional system combines the sum of the decision-making procedures carried out by boards of directors, stockholders at annual meetings, management, foremen, and other employees, with the advice of outside agents such as lawyers, accountants, and public relation persons, which together form collective corporate "intentions" that are exhibited in corporate "decision-making," corporate "action," and organizational goals. Notice that only those intentions of constituents and outside agents that contribute to the corporate decision-making processes count as primary intentions out of which the secondary intentional system operates. This sort of intentional system functions only in terms of the structure of the corporation, its goals, and the selective decision-making processes that are deemed pertinent to corporate activities. Thus a corporation is a selective intentional system, since not all constituent or agent intentions contribute to corporate "intentionality," but only those playing a role in corporate "action."

Because corporations "act" and because corporations are intentional systems, the fact that under law corporations are treated as quasi-persons is not surprising. However, although they indeed have some of the characteristics of persons, they lack the autonomy necessary to perform primary actions, one of the conditions necessary to be ascribed full personhood. This fact and the selectivity of the corporate intentional system preclude its full identification as a person.[6]

CORPORATE MORAL AGENCY AND MORAL RESPONSIBILITY

The description of corporate "intentionality" and corporate "action" is important to develop any notion of corporate moral agency and moral responsibility. Because corporate "actions" are what I have called secondary actions, a corporation is not an independent moral agent. Unlike individual actions, which are presumed to be free choices of autonomous agents, corporate "action" is an outcome of groups of choices of constituents and agents acting on behalf of the corporation. One can say intelligibly that a corporation "acts" only when one means that a corporation performs a secondary action.

Because secondary actions are ascribed to corporation, corporations are often held responsible for these "actions." This is not without justification, because if secondary actions are collective actions, then they cannot be reascribable to individuals whose primary actions were the basis for them. Moreover; because secondary actions are, in a derivative way, actions of persons, they can be moral or immoral actions, and one may evaluate them accordingly. Thus because of their origins, collective secondary actions can be praiseworthy or blameworthy even though there is no Actor-Corporation.

That secondary action can be a positive moral action is illustrated in the Nestle Corporation's recent "decision" (a secondary decision based on a series of primary decisions) to stop marketing infant formula in Third World countries where it had been misused. That corporations in fact *do*

---

[6]In his article, "Vicarious Agency," Larry May argues for a sort of agency for corporations which is not identical to moral personhood and is more akin to legal agency. Since there are difficulties with legal agency as illustrated in the *Bellotti* case, I find my notion of a corporation as a secondary collective more satisfactory for explaining corporate moral responsibility. See Larry May, "Vicarious Agency," *Philosophical Studies*, 43 (1983), pp. 69–82.

"respond" to moral demands is also seen in the recent example of the Johnson & Johnson Company, which reacted to the Tylenol scare by removing that product from the market even though the company was absolutely innocent of any wrongdoing.

Corporations, then, may be thought of as secondary moral agents. This form of moral agency, however, is dependent upon the moral input of constituents without which corporations cannot and do not take moral considerations into account in their decision-making. However, corporations do not always "respond" positively or even negatively to moral pressures, because corporate moral agency is not independent of the moral input of corporate constituents. Moral reactions of persons are necessary (but not sufficient) for collective moral reaction. The kind and degree of corporate moral "action" and moral "response" depend on the kinds and degrees of primary constituent moral actions and reactions. For example, many employees at AT&T do not feel responsible in any way for the alleged discrimination they are supposed to have abetted. Some do not even recognize that there is a moral issue in this case. And thus AT&T as a collective did not initially "respond" morally to allegations about its promotion policies, because at AT&T there was no amalgamation of individual moral indignation that initiated a corporate moral "reaction" to these accusations.

A second reason for lack of corporate moral responsiveness is that individuals within a corporation often adopt the habits and mores developed within the company. If a particular corporation has a "personality" such that it habitually avoids moral decision-making, for example, this attitude could be reinforced by individuals who simply act only within their role responsibilities. For example, the Polaroid Corporation manufactured and sold cameras in South Africa. Without evaluating the positive or negative aspects of its policies, Polaroid initially adopted the work practices of the South Africans. These included excluding nonwhites from supervisory positions, paying nonwhites less than whites for the same work, and segregating washroom and lunchroom facilities. Polaroid simply did not evaluate the moral dimensions of this practice. As a secondary moral agent such moral "aloofness" is possible when constituents are not encouraged to consider moral issues in the collective decision-making process. Only when some black employees at Polaroid's Massachusetts plant discovered these South African practices and protested did decision-making at Polaroid begin to take into account the problems in the African plants. In response to the outcries of its employees, Polaroid investigated its South African employment practices and improved working conditions for nonwhites. But it took persistent constituent activity that went beyond employee role responsibilities to trigger this change in Polaroid's activities.[7]

[7]Charles E. Summer and Jeremiah J. O'Connell, eds., *The Managerial Mind* (Homewood, Ill: Richard D. Irwin, Inc., 1973), pp. 822–70.

Thus the activation of corporate moral decision-making depends on the character of decision-making within a corporation, how individuals within a corporation weigh, or are pressured to weigh, their role responsibilities against a broader moral perspective, and how intentions, role responsibilities, and constituent actions blend to formulate the corporate secondary activity in question. Unfortunately role responsibilities seldom include moral directives. So external moral pressures on a corporation do not always trigger the mix of individual actions that become a corporate moral response. It is no wonder, then, that the corporation is often compared to a machine, because corporations often do act as if they had the moral awareness of Robotron.

Although they sometimes appear to take morally neutral stances, and do not always "recognize" moral demands, corporations as secondary collectives made up of persons *can* "act" as moral agents, and therefore *are* morally responsible. Moral awareness, however, is dependent upon the moral input of corporate constituents. If corporate constituents are rational free adults, and one must assume they are, their crucial input into corporate decision-making is such that moral blindness does not excuse a corporation from moral responsibility just as it does not excuse rational free adults.[8]

CONCLUSION

A corporation is a distinct functional entity. It is an intentional system to which one may ascribe secondary moral agency. A corporation functions only as a result of individual primary actions, but the "actions" of a corporation are not redescribable merely as the aggregate result of these individual actions. Because of the nondistributive character of at least some corporate actions and intentions, a corporation is "something more" than an association or an aggregate, but this "something more" is not a physical, perceivable or even psychic phenomenon. Rather, a corporation functions as a unit, dependent upon, but distinct from, its constituents. Because a corporation is capable of secondary action, it is a secondary moral agent but is not morally autonomous. And corporations, like persons, are and should be, held morally responsible for actions within their control when, all things considered, they could have acted otherwise.

[8]In a recent article, "Why Corporations Are Not Morally Responsible for Anything They Do," Manuel Velasquez argues that while there is a sense in which it can be said that corporations "act," moral responsibility cannot be attributed to corporations, but only to their members (constituents). I find this account inconsistent. If it makes sense to say that corporations act, it also makes sense to ascribe to them degrees of moral responsibility relevant to the nature of the corporate action. (See Manuel Velasquez, S.J., "Why Corporations are Not Morally Responsible for Anything They Do," in *Business and Professional Ethics Journal*, 2 (1983), pp. 1–18.)

3

Rights, Responsibilities, and Corporate Accountability

Corporations have been operating as highly successful economic organizations for some years. The fact that they sometimes do not develop moral sensitivity or take seriously their moral responsibilities is not necessarily offensive to them, for they seldom assert that they are moral as well as economic organizations. Nor have corporations often thought that moral seriousness was necessary for economic success. At the same time, however, corporations in this country argue that they should be as free as possible from governmental regulations and legal interferences, that they are and should be treated as autonomous, independent economic organizations. Corporations, then, are arguing that they have rights, in particular the rights to autonomy and economic freedom. Although they may be demanding only *legal* rights to autonomy, legal rights, as we argued in the Introduction, must have a moral basis if they are to be justified claims. So if corporations claim legal rights to freedom and autonomy, they must claim these are *moral* rights as well. If corporations have moral rights, then they have the obligations connected with such rights, and they can be held accountable, *morally* accountable.

In this chapter we shall discuss the nature of corporate rights. It will be argued that the rights of organizations such as corporations are derived from, dependent upon, and secondary to, individual rights, although they are not identical to them. Therefore corporate rights claims entail obligations to respect the equal rights of other individuals, as well as other corporations. Corporations have responsibilities and should be held accountable for their actions. These include actions entailed by their role responsibilities as productive organizations and by role responsibilities to constituents and to the community. But corporate responsibility is broader than role responsibility, because as secondary moral agents corporations have, albeit derivatively, the capacity to make moral choices. It will be concluded that if the economic freedom so valued in a capitalist economy is to be preserved, and if such freedom is necessary for economic success, corporations need to take seriously their status as secondary moral agents.

DO CORPORATIONS HAVE MORAL RIGHTS?

The fact that corporations are secondary moral agents would seem to imply that they have moral rights. The constitution and scope of collective rights is not, however, identical to the constitution and scope of individual rights because corporations are not identical to persons. Persons have primary moral rights, some of which, such as the right to life, are rights possessed by all human beings; while others, such as the right to freedom, are rights possessed only by autonomous rational adults who are capable of independent (primary) action. The "actions" of corporation, on the other hand, are secondary actions constituted by primary actions of rational adults. Because rational autonomous adults are capable of primary moral or immoral action, corporations are secondarily capable of such "actions." There is thus good reason to speak of corporations as having secondary moral rights, rights that they derive from their capacity to "perform" secondary actions.

Since all moral rights are equal rights, secondary moral rights are equal rights as well, and they, like all moral rights, entail obligations. But the nature of secondary rights is somewhat different from individual or primary rights. Let us take as an example the right to freedom. Because corporations are secondary moral agents, they, like individuals, should have some sort of moral right to freedom. If corporations have the right to freedom, it must be an equal right such that each corporation has the right to be treated as an equal with every other corporation and also the obligation to respect equally the rights of other corporations. No corporation can justify a claim to any moral right without honoring the similar rights of other corporations, and honoring them equally. This follows from our discussion in the Introduction of the obligatory nature of moral rights.

If corporations have rights, they have obligations to respect the equal rights of persons as well as other corporations. So if corporations have the right to freedom, at a minimum they have "duties," secondary duties, to treat persons as well as other corporations as free and equal moral agents. The point is that corporate rights entail duties to individuals whose actions constitute corporate activities as well as duties to other corporations. This is because a corporation's rights derive from, although as we shall argue, they are not merely redistributable to, individual rights.

The most distinguishing feature of corporate rights or secondary rights is that no secondary right can exceed any individual's entitlement to a right. Indeed, the rights of organizations are distinguished from individual rights because, being derived from them, they do not take precedence over, but rather should be secondary to, individual rights. There are a number of reasons for this. Corporations are not autonomous agents. They can neither act independently nor make decisions independently of the choices, decisions, or actions of their constituents, and therefore cannot in a literal sense administer their own rights. Yet the rights that are of most value to corporations, namely, freedom and autonomy, are the very rights normally possessed only by rational adults. Corporations cannot have more in the way of these rights than individuals who are able to administer their own rights. One may make a similar case for claiming that corporate property rights cannot exceed individual property rights since by the same argument the former are derived from, and are not independent of, the latter.

Rights of organizations such as corporations have another distinctive characteristic. They are collective rather than aggregate rights. This is because, if the arguments of the preceding chapter are correct, corporate "actions" and "intentions" are not merely aggregates of individual constituents' actions and intentions.[1] A corporation is an intentional system and can "act;" it is a secondary moral agent, and it can "take moral responsibility." So secondary rights are ascribable to the collective. To reiterate, these are secondary rights derived from and dependent on primary individual rights. But they are collective rather than aggregate rights, because they are ascribed to a corporation, not to individuals or to an aggregate of constituents connected with the corporation. That they are so ascribable is accounted for by the collective nature of corporate "intentionality" and "action," which permits secondary moral agency, and therefore secondary moral rights ascription.

Let us consider an objection to the thesis that corporations have secondary moral rights. Corporations are legal creations governed by the law and by social conventions. It might appear to be the case, then, that the so-called moral rights of such organizations are merely conventional rights prescribed or allowed by the social or legal system in which they operate.[2]

---

[1]This point is in contrast to Robert Hessen's claim that corporate rights are *only* an aggregate of individual rights. See Robert Hessen, *In Defense of the Corporation* (Stanford: Hoover Institution Press, 1980), Chapter 4.

[2]David Ozar, "Do Corporations Have Moral Rights?," *Proceedings of the Conference and Workshop on Business Ethics*, DePaul University, 1983, forthcoming in the *Journal of Business Ethics*.

This is in part true. In the United States, at least, the rights of corporations are fairly clearly spelled out in the law. However, the basis or justification for a conventional right or a right granted by law must be a more general principle, that is, a *moral* right. This point was discussed in the Introduction. What I am arguing is that because of their derivation and structure, organizations have secondary *moral* rights derived from individual moral rights. These should (but do not always) serve as the basis for determining and evaluating the conventional rights attributed to corporations.

A recent case before the Massachusetts Supreme Court clarifies the nature of secondary moral rights, and illustrates the difference between the conventional and moral rights of corporations.

> In *First National Bank* v. *Bellotti* the Court invalidated a Massachusetts statute prohibiting business corporations from making contributions or expenditures to influence the vote in connection with any matter submitted to the voters, unless the matter would materially affect the property, business, or assets of the corporation.[3]

What is argued in *First National Bank* v. *Bellotti* is that corporations have as many First Amendment rights to the freedom to influence voters as persons do. These are legal rights, but they must have a moral basis in order to be justified claims. So if corporations have rights to First Amendment freedoms, these should be based in moral rights, rights that are secondary because of the nature of corporations. Moreover, corporations have obligations. If a corporation demands the right to free speech, as was evidenced in *First National Bank* v. *Bellotti*, it must recognize the rights to free speech of other corporations *and* of individuals, including its employees. Otherwise its demand is not based on a *moral* rights claim. It is inconsistent for a corporation to expect individuals within the corporation to perform the primary actions that constitute a collective corporate free "action" unless they also may exercise that right and exercise it equally. A corporation cannot exercise more freedom than its constituents. At a minimum, corporate rights claims must honor constituent rights claims, and the former cannot exceed the latter.

A corporation, then, cannot legitimately enjoy freedoms not afforded, or not afforded equally, to persons. This point supports the contention we shall defend in Part II that any power afforded to corporations as a result of ownership and control of the means of production does not validate rights that exceed individual entitlements. The *Bellotti* decision is controversial in this respect. It recognizes the corporation as a subject for the right to freedom, but reflects a lack of interest by the courts in seeking

---

[3]Charles P. O'Kelley, Jr., "The Constitutional Rights of Corporations Revisited: Social and Political Expression and the Corporation after *First National Bank* v. *Bellotti*," *Georgetown Law Review,* 67 (1979), pp. 1347–84. See also, *First National Bank* v. *Bellotti*, 435 U.S. 765 (1978).

to balance the rights of organizations and individuals. By reason of their financial resources corporations obviously have greater power to influence votes than do individuals. The *Bellotti* decision by reinforcing this power makes possible an imbalance of individual and corporate voter influence in favor of the corporation, and thus grants to corporations legal rights that exceed their justified moral rights claims. This extension of legal rights to freedom beyond the scope of a moral right to freedom treats corporations as if they were super-persons rather than secondary moral agents. It give to them undue power, power that can be misused to the detriment of individuals.

Finally, the *Bellotti* decision questions the status of a corporate moral right. Corporate moral rights are *secondary* rights, attributed to corporations on the basis of their *secondary* moral agency. But since corporate moral rights are derived from individual rights, and since corporations, unlike persons, cannot administer their rights, corporate moral rights do not take priority over individual moral rights. Indeed, it would be illogical if they could, since they are dependent on individual rights. The individual moral rights of human beings and rational adults should take precedence over collective moral rights of any sort. The imbalance between the exercise of corporate and individual rights created by the *Bellotti* decision, however, grants a conventional legal right to corporations that allows them to override individual moral entitlements for collective rights, a position repeatedly challenged in this book. In general, the difficulty in ascribing rights to organizations and institutions is that one tends to forget the origin of these rights and to regard organizations as if they had the same status as moral persons. Because of this erroneous premise one may neglect to evaluate legal conventions from the point of view of moral rights. Such an oversight may give unequal and greater power to organizations on the basis of alleged but unjustified rights entitlements. The resolution of this difficulty is not to deny that corporations have rights, but rather to emphasize that corporate rights are just that—rights ascribed to organizations created by, dependent upon, and thus parasitical upon, persons.

ROLES, ROLE RESPONSIBILITIES AND CORPORATE ACCOUNTABILITY

As we discussed in the Introduction, rights are tied to obligations. Because corporations have secondary rights, they have duties, some of which are connected with corporate functions—with roles and role responsibilities. A role is defined as "a capacity in which someone [or some institution] acts in relation to others."[4] A role specifies one's social, economic, or political

[4]Dorothy Emmet, *Rules, Roles and Relation* (New York: St. Martin's Press, 1966), p. 12.

functions. Role responsibilities are defined by institutional, societal, and personal expectations. These expectations may be simply stated descriptions of the role or may include normative role models or ideals for behavior. The notions of roles and role responsibilities are related to accountability. One is accountable for an action if one is held liable for that action, that is, if one is held morally or legally responsible for what occurs. In Part II we shall analyze the notion of accountability as it has to do with employee role responsibilities and employee rights. There it will be suggested that role accountability makes sense only when there is recognized reciprocal accountability on the part of the person or organization to whom one is responsible. Here we shall discuss corporate roles and role responsibilities as they relate to corporate claims to moral rights. It will be seen that a correlative relationship is part of what is at stake in corporate accountability, although the relationship between employees and a corporation does not exhaustively define corporate accountability. Corporations are also accountable to their stockholders, to their consumers, to other corporations, and to society. In each case this is a reciprocal relationship, so that stockholders, customers, employees, other corporations, and society are each accountable to the corporation as well. We shall consider each of these relationships.

Corporate Rights and Employee Rights: Responsibilities and Accountability to Employees

Job specifications define the responsibilities of employees at work. These include role responsibilities to perform efficiently and productively in the workplace, not to cause unwarranted or slanderous disturbances, and not to engage in activities that would put the corporation out of business. At the same time these role responsibilities are limited by broader societal considerations, because employees, as human beings, have moral commitments that go beyond their duties to their employer.

Accompanying employee role responsibilities are correlative responsibilities of an employer, that is, a corporation, to its employees, and these are not always acknowledged by employers. As we shall argue in Part Two, these responsibilities are a prerequisite for the development of any moral relationship between an employer and its employees, without which an employee's moral commitment to her employer is weakened. Corporate role responsibilities to employees include, of course, the obligation to pay employees fairly for their work.

In addition, I will argue, corporations have role responsibilities to recognize other constituent moral rights claims. What is interesting is that these are *moral* role responsibilities arising not merely from an employer's legal obligations to its employees. If a corporation does not recognize the moral rights of its employees, in particular the right to freedom, it negates the universality and equality of these as moral rights and brings into question its *own* moral right to exercise freedom. Corporations claim freedoms, such as the freedom to advertise and the freedom to speak out when the government unnecessarily interferes. Forbidding employees to exercise their freedoms is inconsistent since it is upon the basis of these freedoms that a corporation can argue for the exercise of its own freedoms.

Employers in a free enterprise economy claim entitlements to a special right to freedom, "freedom of contract." Freedom of contract accords any person or organization the right to make voluntary contracts or arrangements so long as these contracts or arrangements are freely agreed to by both parties. Employment agreements are commonly thought to be such arrangements, freely entered into by employers and employees. Now employers will argue that employees as well as employers enjoy the right to freedom of contract, because just as employers may hire and fire whom they wish, employees choose their jobs and can quit at any time. An employer who fires someone for justified whistle-blowing, for example, is not interfering with that employee's freedom of contract, so firing does not create an imbalance in the exercise of employee rights. However, freedom of contract is based on a more basic right: the negative right to freedom or the right not to be coerced. A whistle blower who is telling the truth and who has a legitimate case against some activity of an employer is being coerced when forced to leave her job on account of whistle-blowing. Her exercise of freedom is unduly restricted, just as restricted as if, say, she were not allowed to quit that job.

Finally, nonrecognition of employee moral rights is not merely an ethical issue. Such nonrecognition undermines the moral basis for legal claims to freedom of contract. This is because if freedom of contract is merely a conventional right, there is no basis, no philosophical basis, upon which to appeal if that principle is undermined in the law. Therefore a corporation has a great deal at stake in the recognition and/or denial of employee rights. In order to validate and protect its own moral and legal claims so as to carry out its duties to its shareholders, a corporation has role responsibilities to respect the equal rights of it constituents. More will be said about the rights of constituents in Part Two.

Freedom in the Market Place: Role Responsibilities and Accountability to Consumers

The role responsibilities of a corporation to its consumers are spelled out by (1) the corporate charter, by-laws, and goals, (2) the principle of freedom of contract, (3) legal restrictions, and/or (4) societal expectations. They may be specified in other ways as well, but these four are important for an understanding of this aspect of corporate responsibility. First, corporations are formed or chartered for certain business purposes, such as to make automobiles, clean clothes, or distribute CARE packages. These original goals of the corporation are often defined, criticized, and altered by the corporate founders and constituents, and evolve as a corporation changes or as its markets dictate. Whatever goals are in operation set the parameters for corporate role responsibility.

Second, corporations in free countries claim the right to manufacture or provide services, and to market and sell to whomever they please. These alleged rights are ordinarily coupled with obligations generated by role responsibilities for what is manufactured or offered as a service. The justification for free marketing is in part freedom of contract, because it is tacitly assumed that the free marketing of products is acceptable to those to whom the product is being sold and that potential customers are able to comprehend what is being offered for sale.

A manufacturer is responsible for the quality and safety of the product or service rendered. Quality and safety are partly defined by the advertising promises for which companies are accountable, partly controlled by legal restrictions, and partly determined by societal expectations. By "safe" is meant a product that is not harmful when used in the manner intended, and when used according to the cultural mores of the community in which it is marketed and sold. These two criteria may conflict, as some companies have discovered. For example, Vicks Vaporub is marketed in Africa where, to the surprise and consternation of the company, it is eaten as a medicine. This was *not* the intention of the manufacturer, nor was it suggested in their advertising. But as a result of this African habit Vaporub has been made safe for consumption.[5]

Most corporations acknowledge those consumer obligations that are defined by their charter and by the law, but obligations to consumers that are determined by societal expectations or cultural mores are not always fully recognized or are considered less important than freedom of contract in marketing a product. This may be illustrated with the following example.

The Nestle Corporation and other manufacturers of infant formula claim the right to conduct business where and how they please. This right was upheld by the United State recently when it voted against the World Health Organization's condemnation of Nestle's marketing infant formula in Third World countries. To defend itself against criticisms of these marketing practices, Nestle has appealed to its right to freedom of contract. But this is an unjustified appeal since marketing infant formula in the Third World can hardly be said to have been agreed upon voluntarily by the users of the formula. In many Third World countries mothers are uninformed and can neither read instructions nor understand the importance of pure water. That they "voluntarily" agreed to buy the formula

---

[5]Reported to the author by a Vicks African marketing executive. He does not recommend it as a steady diet.

surely stretches the definition of voluntary agreements, which are ordinarily thought of as arrangements or contracts between informed
persons.

If corporations can market their products freely they have role responsibilities to the users, or at least to the "normal users" of their products
as defined by the expectations and the "normal use" of the culture in which
a product is sold. When advertisements show men in white coats recom-
mending a product and it is then sold to illiterate persons who consistently
misuse it because of their cultural norms or economic status, the manufacturer is both responsible for the advertising and, in part, for the subsequent misuse of the product.

One might object that I have gone beyond role responsibilities by
ascribing a broader corporate responsibility to society. Nestles' legal liability, for example, is merely to manufacture a quality product with adequate instructions for its use. Moreover, infant formula has been marketed
successfully in places like Macao, where infant mortality has declined sig-
nificantly because of its use. I would argue that what is required in any
evaluation of a market is not merely whether a product will be used by a
particular group of people but how it will be used. Just because infant
formula was a success in Macao does not guarantee that it will be properly
used in another cultural environment. Not to recognize this is inexcusable
moral negligence. Free marketing depends upon the voluntary acceptance
of products. Marketing products to uninformed persons or to people who
will use the product for a purpose for which it was not manufactured
questions the morality of free marketing, since it allows people unwittingly
to harm themselves. This is not to say that the harm in these cases is *intended*
by the manufacturer or marketer, but that part of the marketer's responsibility must be to consider the economic and cultural mores, and even the
literacy, of the prospective user. At a minimum corporations have the
responsibility not to create harm as a result of their "normal" operations.
Otherwise they would have rights to do what individuals do not: to harm
others for some other end, such as profit. Corporations that do not take
seriously their intercultural obligations threaten their own survival, for
they "exist" only by recognition under the law and could be shut down by a
disgruntled public. This requirement does not make undue demands on
corporations, since such information is normally sought when deciding on
the marketability of any product in a new place. The role responsibilities of
infant formula manufacturers do not extend to the well-being of every
Third World infant. But corporations who sell infant formula to different
markets are accountable for its "normal" misuse in that market, just as
Vicks is responsible for the "normal" misuse of Vaporub.

As is the case with other corporate role responsibilities, corporate
responsibility to consumers implies a reciprocal responsibility on the part
of consumers to corporations. One cannot expect a corporation to be re-

sponsible for its products if consumers deliberately misuse them. The consumer who is knowingly negligent and then returns a product or sues a corporation is not holding up her side of the accountability relation. The plethora of liability law suits against corporations, some of which are on questionable matters, undermines mutual corporation-consumer moral respect and is detrimental to the trust that should exist between both parties.

Ownership, Role Responsibilities, and Accountability to Stockholders

Corporations clearly have obligations to their stockholders, and these are by and large fiduciary responsibilities that arise from ownership rather than from more basic considerations. Persons (or institutions) who own stocks have economic claims against the corporation. The other rights of stockholders, such as freedom, due process, or privacy, are usually not an issue, since stockholders are largely independent from, and are not employed by, the corporations they own. What is seldom mentioned is that stockholders have responsibilities to the corporation, responsibilities few stockholders take seriously. This lack of seriousness has led some economists to point out that we are in a new era of property where private ownership is separated from management and responsibility because, by and large, corporations are owned by absentee shareholders who do not participate in the management or operation of the business, and managed by "hired hands," employees who are responsible for what happens to the company. This is obviously true, but nevertheless as owners, even as absentee owners, stockholders have duties to see that what they own is properly managed. Otherwise they are neglecting all of the obligations connected with their alleged right to ownership. Milton Friedman makes this point and advocates that income tax be abolished and stockholders taxed on the gross earnings per share *before* dividends in order to encourage stockholder involvement in corporate activities.[6]

Friedman's proposal is interesting and provocative because some incentive for stockholder responsibility seems necessary to balance the undue shift of power in corporations to managers, a shift that allows management to do as it pleases even when this is not in the best interest of the corporation or its stockholders. Taxing shareholders on the gross earnings of the corporation is a simple way to revitalize stockholder accountability and interest in corporate business activities. This proposal, or something equally viable, should be seriously considered.

Responsibility and Accountability to Society

The rights and role responsibilities of corporations are defined, in part, by the legal and institutional arrangements of a society. As we said

---

[6]Milton Friedman, *Capitalism and Freedom* (Chicago: University of Chicago Press, 1962), pp. 174–78.

earlier, corporations in the United States are granted charters that give them the right to unlimited life, and they are guaranteed certain of the constitutional rights ordinarily granted to individuals (see Chapter One). Corporations are also heavily regulated. At least eighty-seven different governmental agencies require corporations to fill out over three thousand forms each year. Almost everything a corporation does falls under the jurisdiction of one or more agencies. Because corporations have a second-ary right to freedom, they, like individuals, have a right to object and to hold the government or Congress responsible when regulations result in an unnecessary loss of freedom.

Corporations are members of society, and they expect their rights to be honored. If rights are connected with duties, corporations *do* have obli-gations to the society in which they exist; but do they because of their public (state) charters, have *special* responsibilities to society? This question has been much debated in the literature on corporations.[7] It is often suggested that charters are merely economic conveniences, creating no particular societal obligations. A corporation's sole duties are to its owners and stock-holders. It is indeed sometimes claimed that it is *immoral* to sidetrack stock-holder investments to societal concerns.[8] Such actions are not mandated uses of shareholder capital and therefore constitute misappropriation of corporate funds.

Conversely, it has been contended that because corporations have state charters, they are public institutions rather than merely private busi-nesses. Therefore corporations have positive moral obligations to society, which include the clear-cut duty always to take societal interests into ac-count in their activities.[9]

I would take a moderate position between these views. Corporations obviously have obligations to maximize profits for their shareholders, and as they are usually chartered for economic, not social, purposes, they need not always take the lead in social reform. This is not their purpose. If social reform takes precedence over the economic goals of a corporation, em-ployees are not taking their role commitments seriously enough. However, with this qualification, as we argued in a preceding section, corporations have a responsibility not to harm society in pursuing their self-interests. Corporations have other positive moral responsibilities as well, which entail obligations connected with their operations that go beyond obligations to consumers. If a corporation uses air, water, or natural resources to man-ufacture a product, for example, it is responsible for that use. Since it is

---

[7]See Hessen, *In Defense*, Chapter 4. See also Adolf Berle, Jr. and Gardiner Means, *The Modern Corporation and Private Property* (New York: Macmillan, 1932; rpt. Harcourt, Brace and World, 1968).

[8]Friedman, especially pp. 133–36.

[9]See for example, Ralph Nader, Mark Green and Joel Seligman, *Taming the Giant Corporation* (New York: W. W. Norton & Co., 1976).

using public not private "goods" to its own end, its responsibility extends to respecting these "goods". Corporations must also take a long view of their interests in relation to the community. The well-being of the corporation depends on the well-being of the community within which the corporation operates. A deterioration of that community will surely bring about the demise of the corporation. Long-term self-interests that incorporate community interests are not always present in corporate planning, but such foresight is necessary to preserve the corporation in the society in which it exists and operates.[10] It would be interesting to do a cost-effectiveness comparison of the benefits of plant relocation versus its costs.[11] Setting aside considerations of moral rights, it might be less expensive in the long run for business to contribute to community well-being than to relocate.

Conflicts of Role Responsibilities

It is fairly easy to delineate corporate role responsibilities. It is less simple to resolve conflicts of these responsibilities. A corporation often faces problems when role obligations to two or more parties, such as the shareholder, the employee, the consumer, and/or society conflict, because honoring one obligation may necessitate violating another. These role obligations often appear to be prima facie duties such that conflicts are difficult to resolve rationally by giving preference to one obligation over another. For example, recently the Manville Corporation (formerly Johns-Manville) found itself in a number of role dilemmas. Thousands of its workers had developed cancer or other forms of asbestos poisoning as a result of years of working with asbestos at Manville plants. To honor all the claims of these disabled workers would bankrupt Manville. If Manville were to go out of business, it would neither be able to pay liability claims for its injured workers nor continue to provide much-needed jobs. Workers and shareholders would suffer. On the other hand, not to honor the claims would be irresponsible, particularly because there is some evidence to suggest that Manville had known about the dangers of asbestos as early as the 1930s but

---

[10]For example, the Eli Lilly Company has had its headquarters in the city of Indianapolis for over 90 years. In recent years the neighborhood surrounding Lilly's office and plant has deteriorated. Lilly could have moved out of the community into a safer and more aesthetically pleasing location. But it did not. It took the position that it was more in its long-term interest to improve the community than to move to another place. It instituted neighborhood programs of education, recreation, job training, and housing improvements. The programs have been a success. Lilly is still located at its old headquarters, and the community, while not perfect, has survived and improved. Moreover, the community has supported Lilly's efforts, and mutual relations between the two have flourished. See John T. Moore and James B. Spalding, Jr., "Eli Lilly and Company," in Robert D. Hay, et al., eds., *Business and Society* (Cincinnati: South-Western Publishing Co., 1976), pp. 17–24.

[11]See Margaret Mead, "Social Accounting and the American Dream," in Thomas Donaldson and Patricia Werhane, eds., *Ethical Issues in Business* (Englewood Cliffs, N.J.: Prentice-Hall, Inc., 1979), pp. 233–38.

had neither informed its workers nor taken proper safety precautions then.[12]

Additionally, in the 1940s Manville had another obligation that created a role conflict. Asbestos was a material essential for the construction of World War II ships. During World War II Manville was contracted by the United States government to manufacture asbestos for these ships. At that time Manville was faced with what now are seen as conflicting obligations between protecting the safety of its workers and manufacturing a product essential for the war and hence for the survival of our country. One's initial reaction to this case is to argue that the lives and health of Manville's workers should have superseded other considerations. But in World War II the country counted on our technological strength to win the war, and this depended in part on the use of asbestos. This does not excuse Manville's apparent negligence in not informing its workers and adopting safety precautions, but it shows that in certain situations business responsibilities may lead in conflicting but morally important directions.

Many of the most difficult moral dilemmas facing corporations are role conflicts. It is important to notice that role responsibilities are not simple. They involve moral commitments that sometimes develop into moral dilemmas. The proper solution in each case is, at best, difficult, because as in other moral dilemmas, role conflicts often involve equally viable or equally abhorrent choices, none of which is perfectly satisfactory to all the parties involved. Nevertheless, using the discussion of basic moral rights at the beginning of the book, there are certain principles to keep in mind in settling such dilemmas.

In order of importance these principles are:

1. First, one must weigh the moral rights of each individual involved. These must be respected even at the expense of other, more utilitarian, benefits.

In the Manville case, as in other difficult cases, this weighing does not produce a clear-cut answer. During World War II Manville confronted two conflicting sets of rights: (a) the right to life and health of its workers, versus (b) the right to survival of a nation. It opted for (b) over (a) as if these were mutually exclusive choices and no mediating option was possible. Manville did not consider the second priority in moral decision-making.

2. When there appear to be irresolvable conflicts between equal basic rights, one should seek a compromise that honors each equally, even if not absolutely or perfectly.

[12]See Jeff Coplon, "Left in the Dust," *The Village Voice,* March 1, 1983, pp. 1–34, and "Manville Plans to Seek Strict Limit on its Liability for Asbestos Claims," *The Wall Street Journal,* January 27, 1983, p. 31.

In the case of Manville, which faced conflicts between different claimants of one right, the right to life, providing safety precautions and information to employees during the 1940s could have saved many workers' lives without endangering asbestos production for the war. Creative moral compromise was needed to settle what at first appeared to be an irresolvable conflict of equal basic moral rights to life. In cases where two different rights conflict one always opts for the most basic moral right. Where there is a conflict between two equally valid basic moral rights, one should seek a compromise that respects both as equally as possible.

3. After weighing the rights of each party, and only when these have been weighed, one should opt for the solution that causes the least harm for all parties involved.

By not informing asbestos workers of the dangers of the product and by not instituting safety precautions in its plants in the 1940s Manville did not exercise this responsibility. However, Manville's recent declaration of technical bankruptcy may be an illustration of an exercise of principle 3. To minimize the harm to shareholders, employed workers, and injured workers, Manville chose a compromise solution between the claims of the three parties. Manville is in technical bankruptcy (legally termed "Chapter 11") so that it can stay in business and preserve jobs for its present workers while not having to bear the full burden of the liability suits of injured workers. It has not abrogated total responsibility for these suits, however, because all claims against the company are to be settled by the courts. Ideally, all claimants will receive equal consideration, although there is no guarantee of this. In this instance it may be debated whether or not bankruptcy was the best of all possible options open to Manville, and it may be debated whether or not Manville is taking its full share of responsibility for the injured workers. But one would have to admit that this compromise solution seeks to reduce harm to each party involved. Manville can stay in business, and the courts should distribute equitable awards to injured workers who have filed legitimate claims. This is not a perfect solution; it is a moral compromise that tries to mediate between claims without destroying the practical means of realizing them. The shortcoming of this compromise is that Manville may have tried to reduce harms without taking into prior consideration the question of *rights*.

4. Having considered 1, 2, and 3, and having weighed the moral rights of each party, one may then weigh the benefits of each solution against the possible harms.

Manville chose to declare bankruptcy in order to save itself, preserve employment for its workers, and attempt to honor its moral commitments to injured workers. This is an attempt to balance benefits and harms in a way not totally unsatisfactory, although not perfect, for everyone. So long as equal basic moral rights receive first priority, this is not the worst of solutions. The problem is that in many cases companies appeal to 3 and 4 and neglect 1 and 2. It may be argued that Manville's solution did not give equal weight to the basic moral rights of its asbestos victims. This is probably true. But had the rights of these victims been adequately taken into account, Manville would have been justified in appealing to 4. A better option in this case might however have been for the courts to force Manville to stay in business without declaring bankruptcy until all the suits were settled.[13]

In general, conflicts of prima facie role duties are resolvable. There is seldom a perfect solution that will respect all basic moral rights of all parties absolutely, but if the priority of basic equal rights is kept in mind, and if one is willing to opt for creative moral compromise that respects claims of all parties equally, acceptable solutions to role dilemmas may be found.

THE LIMITS OF ROLE RESPONSIBILITIES

Individual role responsibilities may clash with each other or come into conflict with more universal moral claims. Role responsibilities, then, are limited, and individuals are also accountable to society in a broader way. Because they are secondary moral agents, corporations, too, share some of this sort of accountability. Earlier we argued that corporations have the responsibility not to harm others even in exercising their right to freedom. This notion of accountability should be expanded. Rights are universal, that is, everyone everywhere possesses them and possesses them equally. Any action of individuals or corporations that prevents the equal exercise of moral rights challenges the universality of these rights. Corporations, then, like individuals, are accountable when their business actions interfere with, or prevent the exercise of, basic moral rights.

The nature of this sort of accountability is best illustrated through examples. The Polaroid Corporation stopped manufacturing instant cameras in South Africa after it discovered they were being used to abet apartheid. But for a long time afterwards the cameras were sold to South Africa through a foreign distributor. Is Polaroid responsible for that use of their camera? International Business Machines (IBM) manufactures and

---

[13]This is exactly what a Japanese court decided in the famous Chisso case. Over many years Chisso dumped mercury into a bay near their plant. The dumping contaminated the fish caught by local residents whose offspring later developed birth defects. The court decided that Chisso should be liable for the harm caused to these residents, *and* that the company could not go out of business until damages were adequately paid to all those harmed by the dumping. See *The New York Times*, March 23, 1979, sec. 4, p. 5, and March 29, 1979, p. 15, as reported in Thomas Donaldson, *Corporations and Morality* (Englewood Cliffs: Prentice-Hall, Inc., 1980), pp. 1–2.

markets computers worldwide to foreign governments, businesses, and private individuals. Recently it has been observed that in many countries, particularly in South America and the U.S.S.R., IBM computers are used by governments to track down dissident political figures, opposing party members, and other persons who allegedly threaten the government in power. It has been suggested that companies such as IBM should withdraw its computers from these markets.[14] IBM refuses saying that it manufactures computers not torture chambers. Machines in themselves are not harmful. It is the people who misuse the computers who are to blame. Is IBM accountable? Should they withdraw their computers from these markets?

Notice that in these instances the issue is not merely role responsibility. The corporation's role responsibility to manufacture and sell a useful and safe product to informed users is not in question. Nor are role obligations to the society in which the corporation is chartered or where it manufactures at issue. In these cases exercising "normal" role obligations in a morally proper way clashes with the basic moral rights of persons for whose welfare the corporation is ordinarily not responsible.

From a practical point of view it is probably impossible for any person or corporation to be held accountable for everything that he, she or it does. On the other hand to be morally blind in areas where moral action is called for is inconsistent with the claim that corporations are secondary moral agents. Just as individuals are held accountable when what they know is a right action conflicts with their role responsibilities, so corporations, too, are accountable for their actions when they could have acted otherwise. As secondary moral agents, IBM and other corporations have responsibilities that are broader than their role obligations. These include the responsibility to respect or at least not to violate the basic moral rights of other corporations and other individuals when these are affected by the way the company carries out its role responsibilities. This is not to say that IBM is absolutely responsible for every use of all its computers. IBM's clearest role responsibilities are to manufacture and market good computers. But it is possible to contend that IBM is not totally exempt from moral blame for the *kinds* of uses to which its machines are put, even when these uses are totally out of the parameters of IBM's role responsibilities, especially when the machines are used to harm the *rights* of others. Polaroid has stopped all sales of its cameras in South Africa. It has set a moral precedent that could and should be followed by others, because it places moral rights, the rights of nonwhites in South Africa, before its profits. Thus it puts moral rights first in its priorities.

What is most disturbing about some of these cases is that it appears that the companies involved do not admit that there *are* any moral issues at

14"Would You Sell a Computer to Hitler?" *Computer Decisions*, 9 (February 1977), pp. 22–26.

stake. The development of moral awareness, I am convinced, would be an impetus for corporate moral development that would foster the notion of accountability on all levels of corporate-social interaction so that corporations would begin to take seriously their moral responsibilities on a basic and universal level.

CONCLUSION: WHY SHOULD CORPORATIONS BE MORAL?

If secondary moral agency is attributed to corporations this implies that such organizations enjoy or should enjoy secondary moral rights to freedom and autonomy. These rights, in turn, entail moral obligations and accountability on the part of the corporation to its customers, to its constituents, and to society. When role obligations conflict with each other one must weigh equally the basic moral rights of each party involved before evaluating the positive and negative benefits or harms of alternate resolutions of these conflicts. However, corporations, like Robotron, can function like amoral machines. They need not "adopt" a morally accountable attitude in their relationships or "accept" the fact that they are morally responsible collectives. This is because constituents acting on behalf of a corporation need not embody moral principles in their business decision-making. We cannot contend, then, that constituents acting on behalf of the corporations and thus corporations themselves must necessarily see themselves as moral agents.

The difficulty with corporations adopting amoral stances is that this conflicts with their role as secondary moral agents. Whether or not they recognize themselves as such, they *are* morally accountable for their actions. Corporations cannot make the excuse that they are merely economic organizations, an excuse that is, moreover, actually damaging to corporations because it forces society to regulate them, just as it would have to regulate Robotron, and to deny them the rights these organizations value most: economic freedom and autonomy, rights only due to responsible moral agents. Of course corporations may claim that these are merely *legal* rights, rights granted by our society in despite of the behavior of corporations. But such a position threatens economic freedom itself because it undermines its moral basis. If the right to economic freedom is of value, moral value, in our society, and I suspect that it is, corporations need to become morally answerable agents. For only under that condition does it make sense to ascribe to them moral freedom. Only when they acknowledge their responsibilities as secondary moral agents will corporations be able to carry out their obligations independent of coercive regulation.

Part 2

The Moral
Status of
Employees

INTRODUCTION

We have become a nation of employees. We are dependent upon others for
our means of livelihood, and most people have become completely dependent
upon wages. If they lose their jobs they lose every resource, except for the
relief supplied by the various forms of social security. Such dependence of the
mass of the people upon others for all of their income is something new in the
world. For our generation, the substance of life is in another man's hands.[1]

The modern business corporation as it exists today is a collective. As a
secondary agent it has rights, but these are entitlements grounded on individual moral rights, which are primary and more basic. Part One discussed
some stakeholder claims as they relate to the corporation and to corporate
responsibilities—the rights of consumers, shareholders, and society, applying both deontological and utilitarian rights tests to these claims. In Part
Two we shall now turn to a most important and often neglected
stakeholder—the employee.

The importance of examining employee rights cannot be exaggerated. That this is the case is best demonstrated by examining the status of
the *legal* rights of employees. Despite the fact that the American constitu-

[1] Frank Tannenbaum, *A Philosophy of Labor* (New York: Alfred A. Knopf, 1951), p. 9.

tion guarantees rights to freedom and due process, rights that are the basis for corporate claims to these entitlements, until recently these rights have not always been protected in the workplace. Unless they are protected by specific laws or contracts workers in private industry have no guaranteed due process procedures with which to appeal firing or unfair demotion on the job. Nor are there any guarantees to freedom of expression, even though it is granted in our constitution. The safety records of many companies are questionable, and true employee participation in business is often considered unimportant or even impossible. The reasons for this situation are complicated as we shall see. Simply put, private ownership is traditionally considered so inviolable a right that other constitutionally guaranteed rights are not necessarily protected for workers in privately owned businesses, unless the business is performing a public service. This position was supported by a 1946 United States Supreme Court decision that ruled that the due process clause of the Fourteenth Amendment does not extend to the private sector of the economy unless workers in private industry are performing public functions.[2] Notice that the government and the courts do not *deny* that there are employee rights in the workplace. But the law does not restrain private employers who penalize employees for their *exercise* of rights, nor does the law afford employees any means of redressing these abrogations.

For example, George Geary, a salesman for U.S. Steel, was fired from his job when he protested selling a steel casing he felt was defective.[3] In Michigan a Mr. Sventko was dismissed from the Kroger Company for filing a workers' compensation claim.[4] A similar incident occured at a Motorola plant when an employee was told that it was company policy to fire any person who filed for workers' compensation.[5] In another case in Oregon an employee was fired for serving on jury duty.[6] In New Hampshire a woman, Olga Monge, was demoted for refusing to grant favors to her foreman.[7] In Illinois when Richard Elrod was first elected Democratic sheriff of Cook County, he tried to fire all the Republican employees in his office.[8] A social worker, Daisy Alomar, was dismissed because she refused to change her political affiliation.[9] And at General Motors an engineer was fired for refusing to file false information on a government form.[10] These and hundreds of other incidents that have been brought to the attention of

[2]*Marsh* v. *State of Alabama*, 66 S. Ct. 276 (1946).

[3]*Geary* v. *United States Steel Corporation*, 457 Pa. 171, 319A. 2nd 174 (1975).

[4]*Sventko* v. *Kroger Company*, 69 Mich. App. 644 (1976).

[5]*Kelsay* v. *Motorola, Inc.*, 74 Ill. 2d 172, 384; N.E. 2nd 353 (1978).

[6]*Nees* v. *Hocks*, 272 Or. 210 (1975).

[7]*Monge* v. *Beebe Rubber Co.*, 114 N.H. 130, 136 A. 2nd 519 (1974).

[8]*Elrod* v. *Burns*, 47 U.S. 347 (1976).

[9]*Alomar* v. *Dwyer*, 447 F. 2d 482, 2d Cir., (1971).

[10]*Percival* v. *General Motors Corporation*, 40 F. Supp. 1322 (1974).

the courts in recent years illustrate why the issue of employee rights is so important and controversial.

The lack of employee rights in this country is not equally bleak in all sectors of the work force. At least one-fifth of all workers in the United States are covered by collective bargaining agreements that protect against unfair dismissal and guard rights to grievance hearings and fair procedures. All workers who qualify for union membership are protected from *having* to join a union by the National Labor Relations Act, and none of these workers can be dismissed for any reason connected with any form of discrimination.[11] However, although unions protect the worker against low wages and unfair dismissals, unions are more reluctant to defend workers in the area of privacy rights and the right to free expression. There have even been instances where a union has failed to defend a member's right to free speech.[12] Many workers who are civil servants, that is, persons who are employed by city, state and national governments in what is called the public sector of the economy have, by statute, the right to due process. These employees cannot be dismissed without a hearing or other grievance procedure. According to a recent statistic, at least 16% of all workers in this country fall into that category. In some states employment rights for veterans are protected under the law,[13] But even assuming that the group of workers protected by collective bargaining and those protected by civil service statutes and EEOC legislation do not overlap, only 36% of all employees in this country are protected by agreements or by law! Fully 64% of all employees, most of whom are in private industry (called the private sector of the economy) have no such protection. Again, this statement must be qualified. All employees are protected by statutes such as the Civil Rights Act, which prohibits dismissal for reasons of age, sex or racial discrimination, and the Right to Information Act, which protects the employee against undue slander in employee records and letters of recommendation. If protected employees have such a plethora of rights, however, how can it be fair that others have only a few rights? Employee rights for every worker are consistent not only with the ideal of democracy but also with the fact that some workers are already protected under laws and contracts.

Despite the cases of questionable treatment of employees cited above, it is not true that most employers are ogres. Many places of employment are decent places to work, many jobs are not unpleasant, and many supervisors and employers treat their employees with decency and respect. What

---

[11]See Clyde B. Summers, "Individual Protection against Unjust Dismissal: Time for a Statute," *Virginia Law Review*, 62 (1976), pp. 481–532.

[12]*Donnelley* v. *United Fruit Company*, 190 A. 2d 825 (1963).

[13]Mary Ann Glendon and Edward R. Lev, "Changes in the Bonding of Employment Relationships: An Essay on the New Property," *Boston College Law Review*, 20 (1979), pp. 457–84.

is troubling is not that fair treatment *never* occurs in the workplace, but rather that the *right* to fair treatment and other human rights have not been firmly established in employment. The determination that there *are* these rights is essential in order that one need not depend merely on the kindness of one's superiors for fair treatment, decency, and respect in the workplace.

Whether or not extending *legal* protection of employee rights to all workers is necessary or even desirable will be discussed in the chapters to follow. The point here is that there are unprotected employees who have few avenues of redress when their constitutional or moral rights are violated in the workplace. The reason for this is that the *moral* rights of employees are not always recognized at work. Thus, unless they are protected by law or by contracts, employees' claims to unjust treatment may be ignored as moral claims. Traditionally the only recourses available to employees whose moral rights were abrogated were litigation, unionization, or legislation. But these avenues have failed to establish either legal rights *or* moral rights for all employees. What I shall argue is that employees have moral rights in the workplace, and that the demand for the recognition and exercise of these rights is a necessary part of the demand for a universal respect for rights. Further, the establishment of moral rights for all employees should be of importance to those who oppose expanding the legal rights and legal protections of employees in the workplace, for if moral rights are respected everywhere voluntarily, there is no need to expand legislation to guarantee these rights by legal coercion.

The claim that employees have moral rights in the workplace entails substantial and very specific entitlements. Chapter Four will discuss and criticize a number of theses defending the absence of employee rights, in particular, the Principle of Employment at Will, a common-law principle that protects employer prerogatives in the workplace. Chapter Five will present the theory that employee responsibility and accountability entail rights in employment. Chapters Six and Seven outline specific employee rights: the rights to due process, to freedom, to privacy, to worker safety, the right to information and participation, and the right to strike and to bargain collectively. It will be the position of these chapters that rights can be set aside only for the sake of other equal rights claims, but that rights claims cannot be overridden for the sake of economic interests or general welfare. The concluding chapter of Part Two, Chapter Eight, will argue for a prima facie moral right to one's job as an implied contract in employment. While this is not a *necessary* precondition for employee rights, it is a moral right sufficient to establish fairness and justice in the workplace.

4

Employment at Will
and The Question
of Employee Rights

Let us begin the examination of employee rights by approaching this notion from a traditional capitalist libertarian point of view. We shall consider the thesis that *employers* have moral rights: rights to control employment. In a democratic form of capitalism these rights derive from the rights to freedom, to privacy, to voluntary association, and to private ownership, rights that are the cornerstone of such a system. These employer rights are guaranteed in the law by the principle of Employment at Will, which states that in the absence of a specific contract or law, an employer may hire or fire any person whenever the employer wishes. Employees also have rights in the workplace according to this view, specifically the freedom to choose and change their jobs whenever they wish. Any modification of the present employer-employee relationship, already eroded by court decisions and legislation, would damage the freedom of employers and would have severe negative consequences for the economy. Whether or not any employer, and in particular any modern corporation, holds this view is not at issue. What is important is to examine carefully and objectively the contention that the so-called absence of employee rights in the workplace is not an oversight, but rather a logical outcome of, and positive contribution to, democratic capitalism.

In the second part of the chapter we shall argue that although employer interests can and should be defended, most defenses of the libertarian position are weak if not inconsistent. Granting equal employee and employer rights in the workplace is more consistent with a defense of moral rights, and extends moral entitlements to employees without damaging the principles of freedom and private ownership so precious to free enterprise.

In what follows, the terms "employee" and "worker" will be used interchangeably to refer to any person in the employ of another. For the sake of abbreviating the argument, the term "employer" will represent the person or institution who is in the position to and thus has the power to hire, demote, promote, or fire someone else. In this context "employer" could refer to an individual, an owner, a corporation, a personnel officer, a manager, a supervisor, or a foreman.

EMPLOYMENT AT WILL

The principle of Employment at Will, hereafter abbreviated EAW, is a common-law doctrine stating that in the absence of law or contract employers have the right to hire, promote, demote, and fire whomever and whenever they please. The principle was stated explicitly in 1887 in a document by H. G. Wood entitled, *Master and Servant.* Wood said, "A general or indefinite hiring is prima facie a hiring at will."[1] The term "master-servant," a medieval expression referring to employer-employee relationships, persists in some areas of the law even today.[2] In this country EAW has been interpreted as the rule that employers whose employees are not specifically covered by statute or contract "may dismiss their employees at will . . . for good cause, for no cause, *or even for causes morally wrong,* without being thereby guilty of legal wrong."[3]

EAW has been upheld in the courts of this country as recently as 1982 when the Supreme Court of Hawaii refused to question this principle. In that case EAW was invoked to justify the dismissal of a hotel employee allegedly fired so that she would be unavailable to testify to federal investigators who wanted to find out about the Hawaiian hotel practice of exchanging room price information. Even though the court recognized the abusiveness of the employer demand, the court ruled that the hotel had the right to discharge her "at will."[4] The firing of Daisy Alomar, the social worker, and George Geary whose casing proved faulty were also upheld by

---

[1]H. G. Wood, *A Treatise on the Law of Master and Servant* (Albany, N.Y.: John D. Parsons, Jr., 1877), p. 134.

[2]For example, until the end of 1980 the *Index of Legal Periodicals* indexed employee-employer relationships under this rubric.

[3]Lawrence E. Blades, "Employment at Will versus Individual Freedom: On Limiting the Abusive Exercise of Employer Power," *Columbia Law Review,* 67 (1967), p. 1405, quoted from *Payne* v. *Western,* 81 Tenn. 507 (1884), and *Hutton* v. *Watters,* 132 Tenn. 527, S.W. 134 (1915).

[4]*Parnar* v. *Americana Hotels, Inc.* Hawaii, 652 P. 2d 625 (1982).

the courts on the basis of Employment at Will. It should be noted that other recent court decisions have ruled in favor of the employee. For example, Ms. Nees, the woman who was fired for fulfilling jury duty was reinstated after taking the case to court, as were Mr. Sventko and Ms. Kelsay, the persons who filed worker's compensation claims. Some courts have even overreacted against the principle of EAW. However, in none of these instances has the employee been reinstated on the basis that EAW is a questionable doctrine. Rather it was decided that public policy was violated in each rescinded case.

Defending the Principle of EAW

While the Principle of EAW may appear to be unjust in some cases where it is invoked, it has been strongly defended not only in the courts but in philosophical theory as well. The principle is often justified for one or more of the following reasons:

1. The right to private ownership guarantees that employers may employ whomever and whenever they wish.
2. Employee rights that go beyond EAW often conflict with employer freedoms.
3. EAW defends employee and employer rights equally, in particular the right to freedom of contract.
4. In freely taking a job, an employee voluntarily commits herself to role responsibilities and company loyalty, both of which are undermined by the intrusion of certain employee rights.
5. Extending rights in the workplace often interferes with the efficiency and productivity of the business organization and thus in the long run reduces the benefits of free enterprise.
6. Employee rights require institution by public policy, such as legislation and/or regulation. This spells the end of voluntarism in the marketplace, which is essential to capitalism.

Let us examine each of these arguments in more detail. The principle of EAW is sometimes maintained purely on the basis of rights to private ownership. It is contended that the rights to freedom and to private ownership are valid entitlements, and that they include the right freely to use and improve what one owns, including all aspects of one's business, so long as one does not violate the basic moral rights of others. Whether one defines "basic moral rights" as merely negative rights or as more positive entitlements remains an issue in spelling out the limits of property rights. Traditionally, at least from a libertarian perspective, basic moral rights have by and large been conceived as negative rights. According to this view, because employers have these property rights, an employer has the right to dispose of an employee's work freely because that work changes the employer's production. In dismissing or demoting employees, the employer is not denying rights to *persons*. Rather, the employer is simply excluding that person's *labor* from the organization. Instituting employee rights restricts the employer's legitimate freedom to do what she wishes with her production, thus violating her property rights.

Second, provisions that extend employee rights beyond EAW conflict with or override employer rights. In particular, extending employee entitlements by instituting due process procedures when firing or demoting, allowing freedom of expression when this might conflict with employer interests (as in cases of whistle blowing), or expanding employee privacy rights when information valuable to the business is at stake, conflict with an employer's right to do as she pleases. The employee in these circumstances enjoys *greater* freedom than the employer because the employee can act as he pleases while the employer is restricted by the institutional strictures of employee rights.

This reasoning leads to the third defense of EAW. Contrary to what is sometimes contended, EAW defends employee and employer rights equally. An employer's right to hire and fire "at will" is balanced by a worker's right to accept or reject employment. The institution of any employee right that restricts "at will" hiring and firing would be unfair unless this restriction were balanced by a similar restriction controlling employee job choice in the workplace. Such programs would do irreparable damage by preventing both employees and employers from continuing in voluntary employment arrangements. These arrangements are guaranteed by the right to "freedom of contract," which, one will recall, is the right of persons or organizations to enter into any voluntary agreement with which all parties of the agreement are in accord.[5] Employee rights restrict freedom of contract and thus are clearly coercive, because they force persons and organizations to accept behavioral restraints that place unnecessary constraints on voluntary employment agreements.[6]

Fourth, an employee freely commits himself to certain loyalties and responsibilities when taking a job. This voluntary commitment is threatened by the expansion of employee rights. Extending rights in the workplace implicitly implies that in fact an employee need not be loyal to his employer, a phenomenon which, if true, would mean the end of employee responsibility and accountability as it is commonly expected in employee-employer relationships. More will be said about loyalty and role responsibilities in the next chapter.

EAW is most often defended on practical grounds. From a utilitarian perspective hiring and firing "at will" is deemed necessary in productive organizations to ensure maximum efficiency and productivity, the goals of such organizations. To disrupt this would defeat the primary purposes of

---

[5]See *Lockner* v. *New York*, 198 U.S. (1905), and Adina Schwartz, "Autonomy in the Workplace," in Tom Regan, ed., *Just Business* (New York: Random House, 1984), pp. 129–40.
[6]Eric Mack, "Natural and Contractual Rights," *Ethics*, 87 (1977), pp. 153–59.

free enterprise organizations in a capitalist economy. In the absence of EAW unproductive employees, workers who were no longer needed, and even troublemakers would be able to stay in the employ of a business. Even if a business *could* rid itself of undesirable employees, the lengthy procedure of due process required by an extension of employee rights would be costly, it would be distracting to other employees, thus slowing production, and would be harmful to the morale of other employees. Permissive whistle blowing is especially bothersome, because it calls the employer's integrity into question and may harm innocent workers allegedly involved in the activity in question.

The strongest reason for not instituting a full set of employee rights in the workplace, at least in the private sector of the economy, has to do with the nature of business in a free society. Businesses are privately owned voluntary organizations of all sizes from small entrepreneurships to large corporations. As such, they are not subject to the restrictions governing public and political institutions. Political procedures such as due process, needed to safeguard the public against the arbitrary exercise of power, do not apply to voluntary private organizations. Extending these to the workplace would require public policies interfering both with the right of persons and organizations not to be forced into activities not of their choosing and with their correlative freedom of contract. Thus the institution of a full set of employee rights would spell the end of free enterprise as it should be, because guaranteeing rights in the workplace would require restrictive legislation and regulation. Corporations would lose their freedom. Voluntary market arrangements, so vital to free enterprise and guaranteed by freedom of contract would be sacrificed for the alleged public interest of employee claims. Therefore, according to defenders of EAW, this principle is crucial to preserve employer and employee freedoms, to insure the continued economic success of free enterprise, which benefits employees as well as employers, and to safeguard the voluntarism that is essential to democratic capitalism.

EMPLOYEE RIGHTS AND A REFUTATION OF EAW

The foregoing defenses of the practice of EAW make a number of questionable judgments. First, a defense of EAW on the basis of property rights appears to ignore the fact that employees are persons and thus require, *morally* require, different treatment than robots or property. The argument that EAW is a free, efficient practice of voluntary organizations is also based on the questionable assumptions: (a) that employers in these organizations do not exercise arbitrary power in their positions, and (b) that "at will" employment practices are fair and noncoercive. So EAW may eschew the exercise of freedom in favor of the employer. There is also a failure to recognize that the absence of rights in the workplace puts employees at an unfair disadvantage vis-à-vis other employees, a disadvantage that creates harmful inequalities and thus injustices in the workplace. Let us examine these criticisms.

Property Rights

EAW has been defended on the grounds that every person has the right to own and accumulate property and the freedom to dispose of what they own as they see fit. To say that employers have the right to dispose of what they own "at will" is a legitimate claim that follows from the right to private ownership. But two preconditions for this right are important. First, ownership rights are equal rights. Employers do not, for example, have the right to dispose of their properties if or when this activity violates the equally important rights of employees.

Second, as we argued in the Introduction to this book, property rights are neither basic rights nor absolute rights. In a free society if ownership is defined as ownership of material possessions, then property rights can hardly be rights on the same par with, or overriding, say, the right to free expression in the form of legitimate whistle blowing. This is because free expression, the prima facie right to speak out within the constraints of decency, national security, and the avoidance of slander, is part of the basic right to freedom, even when freedom is defined merely as the negative right to be left alone. Not being able to express oneself and to tell the truth would interfere with one's right to be left alone. In a democratic society property rights are based on the right to freedom, in this case the freedom to acquire unowned or available property when such acquisitions do not harm others. This right too, is grounded on the moral right to the freedom to do as one pleases so long as one does not harm the freedom of others. But because of this, rights to ownership cannot override rights to freedom, because the latter are preconditions for the legitimacy of the former.

Some contemporary theorists will complain that this argument criticizing EAW is based on a seventeenth-century Lockean notion of property and property ownership. The relation of an employer to property today is much different from that of earlier times. Today employers are, by and large, corporations. The corporation is owned by stockholders who have little or no say in the management and hence in the employment practices of the corporation, and is run by managers who hire and fire but who do not own the business and are themselves employees. A defense of employee rights cannot be sustained by criticizing abuses of property rights, but must be argued for on other grounds.[7]

This criticism correctly points out the enormous changes that have

---

[7]See for example George Cabot Lodge, *The New American Ideology* (New York: Alfred Knopf, 1975), especially Chapter 7.

occurred in employer-property relationships. But the evolution of property from single ownership to the corporate arrangement is not fully reflected in the employment policies embedded in EAW. This is because those in a position to hire—foremen, managers and executives—are given the so-called privileges of ownership to treat the noncontractual employees under their jurisdiction "at will" when firing, promoting, or demoting them. The question is, *do* these "at will" employment practices violate the rights of employees? That this is the case will be shown in considering the weakest point in the defense of EAW: the contention that labor is a form of property.

Persons, Labor, Property, and Firing Without Cause

The relationship between a person or an institution and the property he, she or it owns is different from the relationship between a person and his or her work. A person (or an institution) is distinct from his or her material possessions, but it cannot be said that a person is entirely separate from his or her labor. Disposing of the labor of the employee is not the same as disposing of a product of labor or of other property. It is the confusion of these that may be the basis for the allegation that arbitrarily firing employees does not violate their rights. Let us see why this is so.

The distinction between persons and property is sometimes blurred. In a recent article Samuel Wheeler claims that the right to one's own body is a natural property right. One can trade body parts such as kidneys, just as we can trade other properties. And what one's body uses or appropriates, whether it be food, artificial limbs or land, becomes additional property of more or less the same status as the body. Wheeler argues, in brief, that if persons have the right to use and move their bodies, they also have natural rights to unclaimed properties appropriated or transformed by their bodies.[8] If Wheeler's argument is correct, it would appear to support the Principle of EAW. If one's body is a property with the same status as other properties, then labor trades are like other property trades. Disposing of someone's labor is a form of property disposal so that dismissing an employee is as harmful as, say, buying or selling the employee's house.

However, there is something strange about equating ownership of one's body with the ownership of material properties. From Wheeler's argument one could trade one's body by becoming a slave or a prostitute just as one might rent or sell one's house without violating any *rights* because both of these are the same sort of transaction. If a person agrees to become an employee this is a property trade, and the employer can treat the employee as she pleases so long as the employee is free to leave, unless of course the employee has freely indentured herself to the employer. Such

[8]Samuel Wheeler, III, "Natural Property Rights as Body Rights," *Nous,* 14 (1980), pp. 171–94.

indenture, it would appear from Wheeler's arguments, would not violate one's own rights. In all fairness it is hard to imagine that even the severest defenders of EAW would support this principle on Wheeler's grounds.

From Wheeler's argument it could also be implied that a person has the right to everything produced or "transformed" by her body, that is, by her working. In this case an employee would not only have property rights to her job, but would also have full property rights to her productivity in the workplace, to the "full fruits" of her labors. Thus employees would have the right to full payment for the value of their labor input. But even Marx admits that in a capitalist economy no employer can pay the employee fully for her input without going out of business. That employees should get "full payment" for their work is not an absurd position, but capitalist proponents of EAW would certainly not accept this thesis.

To focus on the questions raised by EAW clearer distinctions are needed between the notions of property, person, and labor. In Wheeler's argument and implicit in EAW are confusing uses of the term "property," a word that is applied in a number of senses. Sometimes material property exchanges are wrongly equated with the exchange of labor for remuneration, and the word "labor" can be taken either as the activity of working or as the product of that activity.

The term "labor" is sometimes used collectively to refer to the work force as a whole. Labor also refers to the activity of working. Other times it refers to the productivity or "fruits" of that activity. The latter, the productivity of working, is what is traded for remuneration in employee-employer work agreements. Productivity, labor in the third sense, might be thought of as a form of property or at least as something convertible into property. For example, suppose an advertising agency hires an expert known for her creativity in developing new commercials. This person trades her ideas, the product of her work (thinking), for pay. The ideas are not literally property, but they are tradeable items because, when laid out on paper or on television, they become a form of property and are separable from their creator. But the activity of working (thinking in this case) cannot be sold or transferred. Caution is necessary, however, in thinking of productivity as identical to material property, for there is an obvious difference between productivity and material property. Productivity requires the past or present activity of working, and thus the presence of the person performing this activity.

Person, property, labor, and productivity are all different in this important sense. A person can be distinguished from his or her possessions, a distinction that allows for the creation of legally fictional persons such as corporations or trusts that can "own" property. But persons cannot be distinguished from their working, and this activity is necessary for creating productivity, a tradeable product of one's working. Incidentally, this is

why slavery violates more rights than the nationalization of private property without compensation. Slavery does not merely deny an employee pay in
trade for productivity; it also treats persons as property.

Returning to the principle of EAW, EAW allows the employer to fire
or demote employees without giving any reasons at all. In allowing such
actions this doctrine confuses the activity of working with its productivity.
In dismissing an employee, a well-intentioned employer aims to rid the
corporation of the productivity of that employee. The problem in normal
employment situations is that an employer must also eliminate the employee's opportunity to work at the place of employment, that is, the activity that generated the productivity, and thus must fire persons. So ordinarily when an employer treats the productivity of working arbitrarily
she treats persons arbitrarily as well.

When an employer fires persons without cause or without giving
reason, the employer is presuming that he or she has the right to decide
what should be done to his or her business even when exercising that right
violates the rights of other persons. This presumption is in itself highly
questionable. Treating employees "at will" is analogous to considering an
employee as a piece of property at the disposal of the employer, because
arbitrary firing treats rational persons as things. When I "fire" a robot, I do
not have to give reasons, because a robot is not a rational being. It has no
use for reasons. On the other hand, if I fire a person arbitrarily I make the
assumption that she does not need reasons either. And this logic is faulty,
for if I have hired rational adults, then in firing them I should treat them as
such. This does not preclude firing. It merely asks employers to give reasons for their actions, for reasons are appropriate when one is dealing with
persons. Later we shall argue that employers should have *good* reasons for
dismissing employees. Here the criticism is of EAW's position that employers do not have to give *any* reasons whatsoever. This does not mean
that the employer does not have reasons. He may even have good ones, but
unless he feels morally obliged to state them, he is not treating his employee as a rational adult.

Freedom of Contract and the Equal Exercise of Freedom

Let us examine EAW from another perspective which involves the
notion of freedom. Voluntary private organizations argue that they should
be as free as possible from coercive and restrictive procedures. The requirement of due process before firing might be termed such a procedure
because it restricts the decisions and actions of voluntary organizations by
(a) requiring impartial mechanisms for evaluating employee treatment,
and (b) restraining certain actions of employers vis-à-vis employees, thereby (c) interfering with their freedom of contract. However one needs to
evaluate the role of the employer and the coercive nature of "at will"

employment in voluntary organizations more carefully before accepting that conclusion.[9]

Despite the fact that private employers are independent businesses and employment arrangements are voluntarily entered into by employees, employers are in a position of power relative to employees. This in itself is not a good reason to restrict employer activities. Rather, the possible abuses of this power are what is at issue. By means of his or her position, the employer can arbitrarily hire or fire an employee. Of course the employee can arbitrarily quit too, but an "at will" employee is seldom in a position within the law to inflict harm on an employer by resigning. Legally sanctioned "at will" treatment by employers of employees can, on the other hand, harm employees.

The following analogy illustrates this point. When a business goes bankrupt it is commonly supposed, whether or not there is good reason, that the business deserved this bankruptcy because of mismanagement or some other failing. Persons connected with bankruptcy often have difficulties afterwards borrowing money or getting new jobs because it is suspected that they are bad managers. It is assumed, rightly or wrongly, that the owner or manager in question *deserved* this loss.

Similarly, when one is demoted or fired the reduction or loss of the job is only part of what the employee suffers. It is commonly taken for granted that he or she deserved the demotion or firing, whether or not this is the case. Without a hearing or an objective appraisal of this treatment, an employee cannot appeal if he or she is mistreated, nor has the employee any way to demonstrate to others that he or she was fired arbitrarily or without good reason. Fired or demoted employees, therefore, have more difficulty getting new jobs than those who are not fired, even when the dismissal was unwarranted. The absence of due process procedures in the workplace, in particular those that would afford objective hearings about employee treatment, places an employee at an unfair disadvantage relative to other workers, for those who do not deserve to be fired are treated the same as those who do. That is, it is assumed in both cases that the firing was warranted.

EAW could be defended as the best available policy for protecting the rights of employers and employees. However, this is not the case. The Principle of EAW is to the advantage of the owner or employer and to the unfair disadvantage of the employee, because the employee's so-called "right" to change jobs is restricted by whether or not the employee was fired or demoted, while the employer's right to fire or demote is not constrained. Thus, because of EAW employers can exercise their freedom with

[9]See T. M. Scanlon, "Due Process," in J. Roland Pennock and John W. Chapman, eds., *Due Process: Nomos* 23 (New York: New York University Press, 1977), pp. 93–125.

less restraint than employees, at least in regard to hiring/accepting employment or firing/quitting.

Worse, "at will" practices violate the very right upon which EAW is based. Part of the appeal of EAW is that is protects an employer's and an employee's freedom of contract. It is the contention that instituting employee rights is coercive because this violates freedom of contract by forcing employers and employees involuntarily to change their employment practices. But "at will" employment practices are or can be, coercive. This is because when employees are fired without reason they are placed in a disadvantageous and personally harmful position not of their choosing and perhaps not justified by their behavior. They are forced to find new employment with the stigma of having been fired when their dismissal may have been unjustified. Of course not all fired employees are in the same position. Some deserve to be fired for a variety of reasons. But when an employer need not give reasons for dismissals, there is no way to distinguish those who deserve to be fired from those who do not. The latter, then, may be said to have been coerced, because they are undeservedly out of a job and have no means of redress. According to the principle of freedom of contract, employment agreements are voluntary arrangements agreed upon by both parties. But it is hard to imagine that rational people would agree in advance to being fired arbitrarily in an employment contract. It is, then, difficult to defend "at will" employment practices on the basis of freedom of contract since these practices themselves are, or can be, coercive to at least one party of the "agreement."

If "at will" employment can be coercive, why do persons agree to such employment by accepting jobs? Sometimes a person must take a job for economic reasons, because jobs are scarce, or because his or her talents are limited. In these cases the prospective employee often thinks he is not in a position to bargain for his rights at the time of employment. Sometimes employees are simply not fully informed about their rights as "at will" employees. Often employment is accepted because a potential employee enters into the employment agreement in good faith, assuming good faith and fair treatment in return on the part of the employer. None of these reasons can justify subsequent arbitrary treatment of employees by employers.

These reasons point to the fact that freedom of contract, like other freedoms, is a prima facie right. It cannot be used as an excuse to limit other freedoms without contradicting its own premises. This much is clear from earlier arguments. Moreover, it is also clear that freedom of contract cannot be appealed to as a reason for restricting other employee rights unless the employee was fully informed about such restrictions at the time of employment. This sort of information is often missing in employment agreements. In any case, freedom of contract cannot be used to override another basic moral right even if this should be agreed upon in a voluntary employee-employer contract.

Utilitarian Arguments

"At will" treatment of employees is also advocated as a means of maximizing efficiency. Unproductive or disruptive employees harm business and hamper productivity. A company must have the liberty to hire whomever and whenever they wish. But what is to prevent an employer from hiring a mentally retarded son-in-law or firing a good employee on personal grounds, actions which are themselves damaging to efficiency? Unless they have to give reasons for hiring or firing, there is no assurance that some employers will not misuse their "at will" privilege to the detriment of the business.

Many utilitarians would not accept the foregoing defense of EAW as a good utilitarian argument. They would say that one cannot justify harming someone, in particular restraining their freedom, for the sake of some collective or corporate benefit. Some of these philosophers would make the more restricted argument that one can restrain a person's freedom only if that action would alleviate very great collective or corporate harms, or more narrowly, only if that action reduced a greater collective loss of freedom than the freedom to be given up. Economic harms which affect a large majority override individual claims to rights, then, only in serious instances when these harms endanger societal freedoms. One may use this argument, however, to criticize EAW as well. One could say that abolishing EAW in the workplace would alleviate harms—harms to employees disadvantaged by the absence of rights. While EAW does positive harm to employees, specifically to their freedoms, instituting employee rights would not harm an employer's freedom. Because of the serious nature of this harm to employees, the benefits of employee moral rights outweigh any alleged loss of productivity or efficiency that might result from abolishing EAW. Thus the institution of moral rights in the workplace may be defended from a utilitarian perspective.

Voluntarism versus Public Policy

Finally, critics of employee rights argue that the extension of rights in the workplace requires enforcement through public policy. But this is not necessarily the case. Voluntary institution of employee moral rights in the workplace is feasible and would preclude regulation since it would make public policies unnecessary. Voluntary employee rights programs would, moreover, be consistent with the ideals of democratic capitalism, which defends the cooperative and free institution of equal rights for all persons in all settings. Employers are rightfully wary of employee rights, because they compare our voluntary system to that of Northern Europe where, by law, employees virtually cannot be fired. But this is because European law focuses on *employee* claims while neglecting equal *employer* rights. A voluntary program that institutes *equal* employer and employee rights, one set of rights complementing and balancing the other, would avoid this difficulty. More will be said in defense of this sort of program in the last chapter of the book.

The principle of EAW, then, can neither be defended as a principle that preserves equal moral rights nor on utilitarian grounds. It advocates treating persons as forms of property, it eschews equal freedoms, and is to the unfair disadvantage of the employee. In the next chapter we shall present a positive defense of employee rights.

5

Employee
Accountability
and the Limits
of Role Responsibility

Employee rights have of late become a topic of interest to philosophers and legal theorists, but many writers concentrate on the issue of employee rights to the neglect of the question of employee responsibility. Others focus on the role responsibilities of employees while neglecting the claim that employees have legitimate rights in the workplace. In this chapter I shall show that employee rights, role responsibilities, and accountability in the work place are intimately connected. That employees have role responsibilities and are accountable to their employers is probably obvious. That these are limited responsibilities that can be set aside by overriding moral concerns has been argued in the literature on the subject. What I shall argue is that these responsibilities and the accountability relationships they entail involve reciprocal obligations on the part of the employer to whom one is responsible. If this argument is correct, I shall show that the claim that employees have rights in the workplace is a logical outcome of the reciprocal nature of accountability and the limits of role responsibilities in the workplace. Thus employee rights can be derived from, and follow as part of, employee-employer relationships.

ROLES AND ROLE RESPONSIBILITY

Having a job entails duties, duties incumbent upon the employee. In the workplace some of these duties arise in the context of role responsibilities.

A "role" is "a capacity in which someone acts in relation to others."[1] It defines one's place or function in a social, economic, cultural, or political position. A role can be defined by an ideal or role model—that is, a set of rules or norms indicating how one *should* function or behave in a particular social context. Or a role can describe how persons *actually* behave in these relationships. In an organization role responsibilities can be conceived of as the normal demands of a job, as expectations of the position, as one's individual conception of one's part in the organization, or as the way in which one fulfills or violates the expectations of the organization. Role responsibilities also depend upon the way in which others in the organization perceive their relationship to the individual in his or her role. The demands might be imposed by the job description or by the actions and expectations of other members of the organization. For example, for some time secretaries were expected to make coffee. This was not in the job description, but it was part of the expectations of those who had secretaries. A role responsibility might also derive from one's personal conception of one's position, or from the actions one takes to define one's position. If the secretary sees himself as a potential manager, he will act differently than if he does not. Recently, some secretaries revolted against coffee-making and refused to perform that task. They saw their roles and their role responsibilities differently from the way in which the organization perceived them, and acted according to their own view of their roles.

Roles and role responsibilities have two other important characteristics. First, roles have an impersonal quality. While one's behavior in a role is personal, the expectations and perceptions of that role are impersonal. When one defines a role, such as that of a mother, one gives a description that applies to any number of mothers. When talking about a secretary he is not named but rather identified by his role. He could be any secretary. Second, to add to their impersonal character, roles are defined by implicit or explicit rules, standards, or norms. These rules may be as explicit as civil service regulations or a job description, or as vague and implicit as the duties society expects of a father. The rules or expectations of one's job role are spelled out by job descriptions, organizational rules, the job hierarchy or organizational structure of the institution, by the expectations of the people with whom or for whom one works, by one's own career demands, and even by the mores of society. These "rules" describe both the rights and duties of the role and also may prescribe the ideal role model, the ideal father, for example, or the perfect manager. The role rules, then, are both descriptions and directives for correctness of behavior that give rise to legitimate expectations on the part of others. And it is from these that one defines one's responsibilities and is held accountable for one's role behavior.

---

[1]Dorothy Emmet, *Rules, Roles and Relation* (New York: St. Martin's Press, 1966), p. 12. See also R. S. Downie, *Roles and Values* (London: Methuen, 1971).

Obviously every person has a large number of interacting or inter-defining cultural, legal, professional, and social roles. The secretary is probably a husband, father, son, a member of a church, a card player, a democrat, and a union member. Some philosophers extend the notion of role even further by pointing out that every person has a larger role in the universal human community. This is not untrue, but it is difficult to specify one's rights and duties in this context except in a vague way. This idea will be mentioned again at the end of the chapter. Because of the fact that every person has many roles, because there are often conflicts between different roles, and because of the impersonal and rule-governed character of roles and role responsibilities, it is usually claimed that no person is identical to his or her roles. A person is a free agent who has and can change a variety of societal roles but is not identified merely by his or her roles. Our secretary is not merely a secretary, a father, or a card player; he is a person who can adopt or change his roles.

Role Responsibilities in the Workplace

In a recent book, *The Moral Foundations of Professional Ethics*, Alan Goldman distinguishes two kinds of role models in business and in the professions: a weakly differentiated role and a strongly differentiated role. A role is weakly differentiated if role-related conflicts can be resolved by applying standardly accepted moral principles.[2] For example a secretary would regard himself as having a weakly differentiated role if, when asked to forge a check, he applied ordinary moral judgments in making his decision. In contrast, a strongly differentiated role is one in which certain professional or job obligations outweigh or are thought to override ordinary moral considerations. The actions of Carl Kotchian, the former president of Lockheed, illustrate what Goldman would classify as actions taken according to a strongly differentiated role.

The Lockheed Corporation was in financial trouble in the 1970s. Its president Carl Kotchian went to Japan to negotiate a contract for the sale of Lockheed TriStar airplanes. This contract was crucial for the survival of the corporation, which had suffered serious difficulties and indeed had had to have a loan from the U.S. government to stay in business. In negotiations with the Japanese Kotchian was asked to pay some "pledge money," approximately 12 million dollars, for the favor of receiving a signed contract. About this extortion Kotchian himself says,

> What business man who is dealing with commercial and trade matters could decline a request for certain amounts of money when that money would enable him to get the contract? For someone like myself, who had been

---

[2]Alan Goldman, *The Moral Foundations of Professional Ethics* (Totowa, N.J.: Rowman and Littlefield, 1980), pp. 20–24.

struggling against plots and severe competition for over two months, it was almost impossible to dismiss this opportunity.[3]

Kotchian thought that his role as president of Lockheed was more important than his personal moral beliefs. He felt that as president of Lockheed he *had* to pay the extortion to save the corporation. Kotchian perceived his role as a strongly differentiated one. His role responsibilities outweighed his personal moral reservations, and he felt that this was properly so.

Goldman argues that in business one cannot *justify* strongly differentiated roles, at least not on the grounds of maximizing profits (in Kotchian's case, saving Lockheed from bankruptcy), because profit cannot or should not set aside other moral concerns. According to his view Kotchian's actions in Japan were wrong even if what he did was for the good of the corporation. And as it will turn out, strongly differentiated role perceptions *are* problematic for a number of reasons. Kotchian's case, however, is more complicated than Goldman would allow. Kotchian reasoned that his professional duties outweighed his personal convictions because the consequences of paying the extortion, that is, saving Lockheed from bankruptcy and thereby saving thousands of jobs, outweighed the moral wrong or possible harm of extortion. Kotchian, then, faced two conflicting prima facie duties, one of which was to the moral prohibition against bribery and extortion and the other one to his company.[4] Kotchian judged that the latter duty overrode the former. How he should have resolved this issue will be discussed at the end of the chapter.

A third way that role responsibility operates in the business context may be described as an ethically neutral stance. In the 1970s some men and women had themselves sterilized in order to work with chemicals dangerous to reproduction. Some of these workers did not see any moral implications in this action at all. They merely perceived that part of their job role meant not having children. And in fact it was only when well-meaning outsiders raised the *moral* issue that these and other workers in similar circumstances became concerned about the dangers of working with chemicals and questioned the demands their jobs made on their personal lives. This case illustrates a neutral role differentiated position because the employee sees his job as a role function in a nonmoral context where ethical considerations are not a factor in specifying or accepting role responsibilities.

[3]Carl Kotchian, "Lockheed Aircraft Corporation," *Saturday Review*, July 9, 1977, pp. 7–12, reprinted in Thomas Donaldson and Patricia Werhane, eds., *Ethical Issues in Business* (Englewood Cliffs, N.J.: Prentice-Hall, Inc., 1979), p. 71. Copyright © 1977 by Saturday Review magazine. Reprinted by permission.

[4]See William David Ross, *The Right and the Good* (Oxford: Oxford University Press, 1930) on prima facie duties, especially pp. 19–42.

ROLE ACCOUNTABILITY

Employment role responsibilities are a source of accountability in the workplace. When one has a job one makes a commitment to exchange work for remuneration. It is sometimes considered just to dismiss an employee for failure to perform his or her job even if the employer pays poorly and sometimes even if the employer does not respect other employee rights. The case of George Geary illustrates accountability in the workplace. However unjust the demands of U.S. Steel were in asking an employee to sell a faulty product, there is nevertheless *some* warrant to its demands because the company was trading remuneration for work that was not being done. U.S. Steel was trying to hold Geary accountable for what the company considered a legitimate labor-pay trade. Later in this chapter it will be shown why Geary was justified in breaking the agreement, but here it is important to emphasize that employee rights and role responsibilities contain this element of accountability, an aspect sometimes missing in descriptions of employee rights.

The notion of accountability as it is important in the context of roles and role responsibility is defined as follows.

> When one is accountable for an action one is held liable to answer for responsibilities acquired by one's role, one's office, one's associations, station or situation. Role accountability defines a narrower range of obligations than role responsibility—only those responsibilities for which one is held liable.

For example, a tennis teacher is responsible for giving lessons and improving the tennis of her pupils. She will be held accountable or liable for being on time and for giving a full hour of lesson, but only rarely will she be held accountable for the quality of her pupil's improvement.

Role accountability might also be a collegial obligation—an obligation one acquires by belonging to a group, club or association. For example, union members have certain obligations to the unions of which they are members. These obligations are similar to role duties in that they stem from a socially defined position, but the binding force of such liabilities is sometimes weaker than in job role accountability because membership is more voluntary in nature and one's duties are not so seriously considered.

Reciprocity and Role Accountability

Role accountability and collegial obligation are usually described only as first-party duties of persons to other persons or to organizations. However, this sort of description is incomplete. There are, in addition to these, duties on the part of the person, group or institution to whom one is accountable. These obligations arise in part from the role responsibilities of the party to whom one is answerable, in part from the definition of one's own role, and in part because of the nature of the relationship. These duties, which are second-party duties, are taken for granted or even forgotten except when circumstances challenge their existence. Often neglected in an analysis of accountability, they are reciprocal or correlative obligations implied by role responsibility. And this notion of reciprocity, I shall argue, is crucial to an understanding of the notion of role accountability.

The notion of reciprocity in any social relationship is grounded on the very basic fact that each party in such a relationship is a person or a group constituted by persons. One way to acknowledge this is for each party to treat the other as a rational autonomous adult.

> Reciprocity may be defined as a social relation among agents in which each recognizes the other as an agent, that is, as equally free, and each acts with respect to the other on the basis of a shared understanding and a free agreement to the effect that the actions of each with respect to the other are equivalent.[5]

This does not mean that each party should treat the other in the same way, but rather that each should treat the other with equal respect and as equal possessers of rights and benefits. Because they are social relationships between persons or between persons and institutions developed by persons, accountability relationships entail this notion of reciprocity.

Reciprocity in accountability relationships operates in part, as follows. If I am to justify my actions to a certain group or institution because of my role in that group or institution, this accountability implicitly assumes a reciprocal accountability to me on the part of the institution to whom I am answerable. And if no such reciprocal obligations exist or if they are not respected, my accountability to that individual, group, or institution becomes questionable. I shall explain why this is so. First, it will be useful to examine a distinction that may exist between two kinds of accountability: legal accountability and moral accountability. As an American citizen I am expected to pay income tax on my earnings, and I am held accountable for my income tax return which justifies these payments. This answerability is a legally enforced obligation, that is, a legal liability. Let us suppose that I am an engineer. As a tax-paying engineer and a member of the American Society of Mechanical Engineers (ASME), I am accountable for being honest and competent and for upholding certain ethical principles spelled out in the ASME code of ethics. Both paying taxes and adhering to a particular code of ethics are role liabilities, but the latter is a collegial obligation because I voluntarily join, and can resign from, the ASME. Unlike taxing bodies, professional societies can only punish members in ethical rather

[5]Carol Gould, "Economic Justice, Self-Management, and the Principle of Reciprocity," presented at the Ninth Plenary Session of the American Section of the International Society for Philosophy of Law and Social Philosophy, Gainesville, Florida, January 1983, publication forthcoming in *Economic Justice* (Totowa, N.J.: Rowman & Allanheld). Used with the permission of the author.

than legally enforceable ways. For example the ASME can recommend but not enforce the firing of one of its members from a job if the member is not performing in an ethically acceptable manner. If I am tired of paying U.S. taxes I can of course become an expatriate, but so long as I reside in the United States I can be forced to pay taxes. Because of the enforcement factor one must distinguish legal accountability from moral accountability.

While differences exist between moral and legal answerability, these two forms of accountability exhibit one common characteristic: both involve reciprocal first- and second-party obligatory relationships. This is because both are relationships between persons, or between persons and social institutions. So both entail moral responsibilities on the part of each party to the other. This sort of relationship is evident in the foregoing examples. In legal accountability the reciprocal obligations of taxing bodies to taxpayers are obvious. One's accountability to the taxing body is based on the assumptions that taxes are necessary, that everybody will receive equal treatment from the federal taxing agents, and that revenues will not be misused. When one side of this two-party answerability breaks down the other party's sense of obligation often weakens as well. When taxing bodies misuse funds, for example, taxpayers may feel less obligated to be fair in their tax payments, or they may respond with legislation such as California's Proposition 13.

Turning to moral accountability, the ASME's right to hold their members accountable is based on the collegial obligations of members to that association. But it is also the case that the ASME is, and should be, held accountable to its members. Part of this reciprocal accountability of the ASME to its members is to uphold the ASME standards by reprimanding offenders. But these actions should be taken not merely to enforce the accountability of offenders to the ASME code of ethics, for the ASME is more than a police force. Rather, the organization has a collegial obligation to all members, part of which is to defend their rights. Perhaps it is in part because some professional associations have failed in their reciprocal collegial obligations that many members have not taken their own role obligations to associations seriously.

Can all role accountability be described in terms of reciprocal or correlative relationship? It has sometimes been argued that moral accountability cannot be merely thought of as a reciprocal relationship because the notion of correlative responsibility is defined only in contractual relationships such as those that may exist between buyers and sellers. A contract implies that all aspects of the relationship are, or can be, definite. Often, however, role liabilities are more open-ended. Most hierarchical relationships, such as parent-child relationships, for example, are noncontractual. But the reciprocal relationship implied in accountability *is* evidenced in hierarchical accountability relationships. When parents mistreat children (who did not choose to be children), the children are justified in complaining; and when a child misbehaves the parents have similar rights. The specific basis for such protests is different in each case, and sometimes the particular rights and obligations are not well-defined. In the case of children, the child's right to complain is clearly justified even though she herself may not understand the warrant for the complaint. But in general such protests are justified because these are social relationships. What I am suggesting, then, is that reciprocal obligation is an important element in a variety of accountability relationships: legal, moral, hierarchical, collegial. Although the obligations are not necessarily contractual, the strength of first-party role liabilities or collegial obligations depends at least in part on the equally strong, though obviously not identical, role obligations of the second party to the first.

The argument justifying the existence of reciprocity in role account-ability might be stated this way. The role expressed in a collegial obligation defines not only the place of the accountable person in a group, but also it spells out the place of the group in the life of that person. In being held answerable I must justify my actions within a certain context. This context includes certain at least implicit benefits derived from the role, benefits that translate into second-party obligations of the group to whom I am answerable. Therefore reciprocity is an assumed part of role account-ability.

It has been claimed by Iredell Jenkins that

> accountability must bear the heaviest burden in the effort to instill values and ideals, maintain standards, secure order, and assure cooperation in social life. . . . Accountability should function in two ways and serve two ends: every such group should instill in its members a sense of loyalty to its code, and it should hold them accountable (answerable) for violations of this code.[6]

Let us agree that role accountability is important, and grant my point that accountability involves not merely first-party collegial or role obligation enforced by the group to whom one is answerable, but also entails re-ciprocal obligations of groups to their members or of employers to em-ployees. Then problems occasioned by accountability are not only caused by failures of collegial obligation or lack of group enforcement of these obligations, but also in part by the fact that groups do not always uphold their role responsibilities to their members. And this latter failure has the effect of weakening the collegial or role obligation by diminishing the loyalties of those being held accountable. George Geary felt little loyalty to his employer when he brought U.S. Steel to court, because by attempting to persuade Geary to sell a faulty product, U.S. Steel did not uphold its

---

[6]Iredell Jenkins, "Responsibility, Liability and Accountability," University of Texas, November 6, 1980, forthcoming in *Proceedings of the American Section of the International Association for Philosophy of Law and Social Philosophy.*

obligations to him. Similarly, when employees strike they usually allege that their employer has not upheld her part of an agreement. Striking, then, can be a means to hold the employer reciprocally accountable to workers.

What this analysis of role accountability means for the workplace is that in taking a job employees assume responsibilities connected with that job, responsibilities often only implicitly stated in a verbal contract with the employer. The employee is liable for the terms of the agreement and for exchanging a certain quantity and quality of work, for in demanding employee rights one cannot forget that at the same time one is accountable for certain work specified by the role assigned. This sense of accountability is the other side of employee rights and should not be neglected.

At the same time accountability is not limited to the first-party duties of employees to employers, but also requires reciprocal obligations on the part of the party to whom one is accountable. The justification for demanding reciprocal accountability is that employee-employer relationships are social relationships between persons and groups of persons, as well as contractual ones, voluntarily entered into and freely dissolvable by both parties. If employees are accountable to their employers, then the employer, in our society usually a corporation, is also accountable for upholding its part of the agreement by being accountable in return, albeit in a different way, to its person-employees.[7]

Reciprocity and Employee Rights

The reciprocal nature of employee-employer relationships in the workplace entails some important employee rights, in particular, I shall argue, the rights to fair treatment and respect. This is because if accountability in the workplace is a two-way relationship, both parties must meet their obligations. If this is not the case, the relationship loses its moral justification. If an employee is expected to "act solely for the benefit of the principal . . . and not to act or speak disloyally . . . ,"[8] the employer has a duty to treat the employee with similar respect, for if respect is not mutual, accountability is unjustified.

What constitutes fair treatment and respect? Obviously, fair pay in exchange for work is an essential part of just treatment in the workplace. This exchange is commonly recognized. Indeed it is often considered the *only* obligation of an employer to an employee. But since in addition to working employees are expected to respect and be fair to their employer,

---

[7]See Carol Gould, "Economic Justice." Gould's notion of reciprocity is strongly linked to a notion of equality of relationships, while my notion is more closely related to the idea of equal consideration.

[8]See *Restatement (Second) of Agency* (1958), 385(1). The Restatement qualifies this remark by further stating that "the agent is also under a duty not to act or speak disloyally . . . *except* in the protection of his own interests or those of others. . . ." *Restatement*, 387, my italics.

employers have reciprocal obligations that go beyond fair pay. Employer "loyalty" includes respect for employee privacy, for worker safety, for employee information, and for due process in the workplace.

Specifically, if an employee is to respect his or her employer and the decisions of that employer, the employer needs to honor the privacy of the employee as a human being. Thus the employer needs to treat with confidentiality personnel information and to respect the privacy of the employee's activities outside the workplace. There are at least two reasons for this. First, since employment agreements are reciprocal, an employer cannot expect respect for his or her privacy, that is, respect for corporate secrets, unless he in turn respects the privacy of his employees. The second justification lies in the primary right of persons to autonomy. Disrespecting that right is equivalent to disrespecting employees as persons.

Respect for the employee also entails maximizing worker safety and providing information about unavoidable hazards in the workplace. Expectations of loyalty and obedience are unjustified if one does not protect workers' physical well-being, for like the right to privacy, the right to safety derives from a basic moral right, the right to life and to survival. Not honoring that right is paramount to questioning the status of employees as human beings. More will be said about this in Chapter Seven.

Respect for the employee also entails keeping the employee well-informed about his or her job, the quality of his or her work, and the stability of the company. This information is required because employees are persons and persons should retain control of their lives. Only with accurate information about the place of employment can an employee make informed decisions about the future. One cannot be expected to be committed to an employer if one is ill-informed about one's job, the status of one's position, or the economic situation of the employer. This is not to say that an employer is a welfare agency responsible for every aspect of his or her employees' lives, but the employer *is* responsible for the decency and the safety of the work situation and should enable the employee to improve, if possible, those aspects of her life that are under the employer's control.

A very important employee right entailed by the correlative nature of accountability is the right to due process. Due process in the workplace means any procedure by which an employee *or* an employer can appeal a decision in order to get an impartial evaluation of that decision. An employer has the right to dismiss any employee who does not meet work expectations. However, because the employer has demanded loyalty and respect, the reciprocal nature of employment warrants the employee's demand for equal respect and fair treatment. If he or she feels unfairly treated or dismissed, he or she has the right to demand due process. For due process demands not that employees not be dismissed, but rather that employer actions meet impartial standards of reasonableness, the same sort of reasonableness expected of employees.

The employee rights we have just enumerated, the rights to privacy, to worker safety, to employee information, and to due process, are moral rights that result from role accountability in the workplace. The specific content of these rights needs to be spelled out, a task for the other chapters in this part. What is important in this chapter is to see that employee rights are a logical extension of role accountability and that one can morally justify the demands of role responsibilities *only* by honoring these rights as well. Because they are moral rights, employers are not legally obliged to respect employee rights, but in not doing so an employer undermines the moral justification for employee accountability in the workplace.

THE LIMITS OF ROLE ACCOUNTABILITY AND ROLE RESPONSIBILITY

The foregoing analysis rests on a definition of accountability as role liability or collegial obligation. In this part of the chapter I want to question the completeness of a definition that is limited to these aspects, a discussion that will bring out the limits of the notion of role responsibility as well.

Let us return to the Lockheed Corporation and the problem of its former president, Carl Kotchian. After spending eighty days in Japan and involving Lockheed in serious extortion payments to the Japanese government, Kotchian got a contract of 420 million dollars from Nippon Airlines. This contract was instrumental in enabling Lockheed to stay in business, it provided jobs for thousands of workers, and it helped to pay off Lockheed's government guaranteed loans. Today Lockheed is a thriving company. But Carl Kotchian is not with Lockheed. He was fired. What happened was that the Japanese people found out about the extortion, and the Securities and Exchange Commission found out about the payments. Apparently the Japanese do not look kindly on "sensitive payments." They dismissed the prime minister involved in this scheme (he has recently been convicted of extortion), put other persons in jail, and have been reluctant to give Lockheed any new contracts. The SEC determined that the bribery and extortion were immoral and therefore illegal. Because of his essential role in these matters, Kotchian was fired from Lockheed, even though he had been doing his job and doing what he thought was best for Lockheed at the sacrifice of his own moral beliefs. In other words, even though Kotchian was carrying out his role responsibilities in exemplary fashion, defending what he perceived to be the interests of his corporation, the corporation did not uphold its responsibilities to him. Why was Kotchian accountable for his extortion activities even when they fell within his role responsibilities? Why was he fired?

A second example. A few years ago the Goodrich Corporation bid for and received a contract for an aircraft brake which, they discovered in testing, they had misdesigned. The engineers of the brake tried to cover up its shortcomings by falsifying engineering reports. This case illustrates a number of role conflicts. First, the engineers discovered a conflict between their roles as Goodrich employees and their responsibilities as members of society, since it became clear that to manufacture this brake would endanger many lives. There was also a conflict between the engineers' loyalty to Goodrich and their accountability to professional engineering norms that require, at a minimum, competent engineering procedures and honest reporting. In this case the engineers were caught between three conflicting role obligations, (1) to Goodrich, (2) to their profession, and (3) to persons having to fly airplanes served by these brakes. Liabilities connected with role responsibilities are not enough to explain how, in each case, the actors might be held accountable.

I do not mean to imply that Kotchian or the engineers at Goodrich should or should not be held accountable. But the examples illustrate how complicated the question of answerability can become when there is an inconsistency of expectations, when roles or duties conflict with each other, or when one's role liabilities are incompatible with societal responsibilities for which one might be answerable. In these instances one cannot justify a decision merely by appealing to collegial obligation or role responsibility. Because one must judge competing claims of answerability the decision-making process goes beyond, and even brings into question, role liabilities. Earlier it was argued that role accountability is weakened when persons, groups, or institutions to whom one is accountable do not honor a reciprocal obligation. Here I am claiming further that role accountability becomes weakened and indeed the status of one's role comes into question when there are conflicts between role obligations, between one's role and one's rights, or between one's role and broader moral claims. These kinds of circumstances, then, point to the limits of role accountability.

Despite these limits, our examples illustrate that a sense of accountability persists. Both Kotchian and the Goodrich engineers were accountable for certain obligations that were not merely collegial or role related. The engineers and other employees at Goodrich were accountable because by confusing role liability with broader, more basic moral answerability they neglected their responsibility for the lives their acts affected. Kotchian was answerable not merely to Lockheed but to the Japanese and to societal principles prohibiting extortion. His prima facie duties must be reevaluated not merely in terms of his role responsibilities, but also in terms of his larger obligations to society.

Although role accountability is too narrow a notion to describe all instances of answerability, one must also take care not to blunder on the side of too broad a definition. One is tempted to argue that because each of us is human, each individual, and each group or institution made up of individuals, is accountable for all other human beings. No one would deny that the individual has responsibilities toward the world community, but this is surely too vague a statement to be of much use. Is the World War I manufacturer of railroad cattle cars responsible for their use in World War II as human carriers? Is Kodak accountable for pornographic pictures taken by private citizens? What are the limits to accountability?

In each of the examples cited the actor was held accountable for obligations that were within his or her capacity to honor. These obligations arise from, but often conflict with, role actions. A person, group, or institution is accountable, then, only for the actions that are within its capacity.[9] For example, Kotchian cannot be held answerable for the totality of multinational corporate bribes, but it was within his capacity to stop *certain* payments to the Japanese. Broader societal accountability can also arise because persons have certain rights. The right to life, for example, confers an obligation to extend or at least not to deny that right to others, even when extending this right conflicts with a role obligation as in the Goodrich case. Role obligations, then, and the accountability they demand are circumscribed by the range of one's capacities and abilities and by one's obligation to respect the rights of others.

In summary, role responsibility is a limited concept useful for describing certain social and institutional obligations, but not useful as an absolute criterion for making ethical judgments. As applied to the workplace, it defines reciprocal responsibilities between persons, between persons and institutions, or between institutions. But in the broader scheme, persons and institutions are accountable for more than their role responsibilities. They must answer to one another and to more basic moral principles.

ROLE RESPONSIBILITIES, ACCOUNTABILITY, AND EMPLOYEE RIGHTS

What does the conclusion that role responsibility and role accountability are limited concepts have to do with employee rights? One difficulty with the assignment or acceptance of role responsibilities in the workplace, as we have seen, is that these are sometimes perceived as strongly differentiated or even as ethically neutral. Such perceptions may lead one to act in the workplace against one's own ethical standards and sometimes in violation of commonly espoused human rights. The justification for strongly differentiated role responsibilities neglects the broader accountability to which every individual is subject. A strongly differentiated position asserts that professional or business demands are themselves overriding moral demands, demands that may and should, in crucial cases, take precedence

[9]See Evan Fales, "The Ontology of Social Roles," *Philosophy of the Social Sciences,* 7 (1977), pp. 39–61; R. S. Downie, "Social Roles and Moral Responsibility," *Philosophy,* 39 (1964), pp. 29–36; Charles W. Blatz, "Accountability and Answerability," *Journal of the Theory of Social Behavior,* 2 (1972), pp. 101–20.

over other moral claims. According to this line of reasoning one could even rationalize threats to human lives, as in the Goodrich case, when they result in economic benefits.

An ethically neutral interpretation of role responsibilities is an even less tenable position. This position assumes that moral principles can be bracketed or do not count in the workplace at all. If this were the case there would be no basis for demanding employee adherence to role responsibilities, for no moral obligations can logically be justified in a situation where ethical principles do not operate. Since an ethically neutral position undermines the basis for demanding employee loyalty and obedience, to expect employees to adopt such a stance is inconsistent with other employer expectations.

However, if employees have only weakly differentiated role responsibilities, and if, in a more general way, every person is accountable within his or her capabilities to meet societal moral obligations and not to cause societal harm, then employees have obligations to act in ethically responsible ways in the workplace. From these obligations employees derive the rights to object to participating in, and to protest against morally or legally irresponsible activities when they occur in the workplace. These rights include the right to conscientious objection, the right not to be harrassed or "punished" for speaking out or blowing the whistle, and even the right to strike when asked to perform illegal, immoral, and/or socially dangerous jobs, or when such practices occur in the workplace. These employee rights are entailed by the accountability of every person to society, and they need to be safeguarded in the workplace in order for employees to be able to meet these broader societal obligations.

CONCLUSION

Employee rights logically and naturally evolve from demands for employee responsibility, loyalty, and respect. To deny employee rights in the workplace is to question the claim that employees can be held answerable to their employers. If employees have role responsibilities and are accountable to their employers, this role accountability is a correlative notion which entails the recognition of employee rights to respect and fair treatment in the workplace. Examples of these rights include employee rights to due process, to privacy, to safety, and to information in the workplace. However, we have argued that role accountability is a notion limited by broader responsibilities to society. In order to carry out societal obligations, employees have the rights to freedom and to conscientious objection in the workplace. Role responsibility and accountability lose their status as overriding moral demands once they are understood in the context of reciprocity that constitutes *both* employee and employer rights. It remains in the next chapters to develop the nature and content of these entitlements.

6

Political Rights
in Employment:
Due Process,
Freedom, and Privacy

In 1981 the Supreme Court of the State of Illinois made what should prove to
be a landmark decision. It said that an employee of International Harvester
Corporation, Ray Palmateer, was wrongly fired for supplying information to
local police about employee theft at International Harvester. The company
had tried to justify its firing of Palmateer on the basis of the principle of
Employment at Will. The alleged theft involved a $2 screwdriver, and the
company felt it could handle petty theft as a personnel problem without
involving public officials. However the court ruled in favor of Palmateer, in
part because the retaliatory discharge of Palmateer was in violation of public
policy. The court said, "There is no public policy more important or more
fundamental than the one favoring the effective protection of the lives and
property of citizens."[1]

The Palmateer decision is a landmark decision, because it reverses the
standing tradition in the law that employer wishes take precedence over
employee rights in the workplace. The case indicates a changing view toward employee rights in this country—a recognition that employees or
workers have certain claims even though they are working for someone
else.

We have argued that EAW is an inconsistent doctrine. Because employment arrangements are reciprocal relationships between persons, em-

---

[1]*Palmateer* v. *International Harvester Corporation,* 85 Ill. App. 2d 124.

ployees have at least prima facie moral rights in the workplace. The most important employee moral rights are the basic moral rights we discussed in the Introduction to the book. In this chapter we shall discuss these rights, some of which are politically guaranteed by the Constitution and the Bill of Rights, but which are not always protected in private places of employment. These are: the right to due process, the right to freedom, and the right to privacy.

In the law, interestingly enough, courts traditionally have recognized the right of corporations to due process[2] and to free speech[3] while by and large upholding the principle of Employment at Will for employees. If corporations have these rights—and this is the basis for corporate legal rights claims—then one would expect that employees, rational adults who supposedly have at least equal moral status as rights-holders, would also have them. But this is not always the case. The justification put forward for this inconsistency is the allegation that since corporations are public entities acting in the public interest, they, like persons in the public areas, should be afforded the right to due process and freedom of speech. Persons in private employment not in the public interest, on the other hand, have freely chosen their jobs and can leave whenever they wish. At a private workplace employees are not subject to the same principles as in the public domain. This is essentially an appeal to the right to privacy: at home one may do as one wishes, but in public one's activities are restricted by the rights of others. By analogy, what goes on in a privately owned business or corporation is out of the public domain of jurisdiction. Thus rights that hold in public such as political rights to free speech, privacy, and due process do not apply in the private domain.[4]

However, if the arguments in the preceding chapters are not incorrect, due process, freedom of expression, and privacy are employee rights generated from employer-employee moral accountability relationships. Granting moral rights in the workplace is consistent with granting rights to corporations, and in fact it is inconsistent *not* to do so since, as we argued in Part I, corporate moral rights are secondary rights in the first place. Corporate *legal* rights sometimes extend beyond individual constitutional rights, but this puts them on shaky ground because there can be no *moral* justification for such an extension. But what sorts of rights are due process, freedom and privacy in the workplace, and what kinds of restrictions, if any, should one place on them? We shall now turn to these questions.

---

[2]See *Minneapolis & St. L. Ry.* v. *Beckwith*, 129 U.S. 26, 28, 36 (1889). Charles R. O'Kelley, Jr., "The Constitutional Rights of Corporations Revisited: Social and Political Expression and the Corporation after *First National Bank* v. *Bellotti*," *Georgetown Law Review*, 67 (1979), pp. 1347–84.

[3]*First National Bank* v. *Bellotti*, 435 U.S. 765 (1978).

[4]*Marsh* v. *State of Alabama*, 66 S. Ct. 276 (1946).

THE RIGHT TO DUE PROCESS

Due process is a means by which one can appeal a decision in order to get an explanation of that action and/or a disinterested, objective, or fair judgment of its rightness or wrongness. In the context of the workplace due process is, or should be, a formal procedural right—the right of employees and employers to grievance, arbitration, or some other appeals procedure to evaluate an employer's decision in firing, promotion, or demotion, or to judge questionable activities of employees. Procedural due process in the workplace should not be confused with what might constitute substantive grounds for dismissal or demotion. It is not, and need not be, a right to specific entitlements, such as to free expression, to privacy, etc. Due process, as it will be discussed in this section, is meant to insure fair procedures but not to rule out firing or demotion.

The right to due process in the workplace simply reiterates the constitutional entitlement that every accused person has to a fair hearing and an objective evaluation of his or her guilt or innocence. At a minimum, it gives one a right not to be demoted or fired without a hearing or some other grievance procedure. Granting due process in the workplace is contrary to the Principle of EAW, which contends that an employer need not give reasons for employment practices. But due process is consistent with the democratic ideal that guarantees the universal right to fair treatment, since without due process, we will argue, an employee does not receive fair treatment in the workplace. Notice that "fair treatment" is not equivalent to *identical* treatment. Just as murderers do not deserve the *same* treatment as nonmurderers, so too, poor employees do not deserve the same job security as good ones. But every person—murderer, drunk, sloth, or loyal employee—deserves a fair hearing to prove his or her guilt or innocence in the workplace. Procedurally, due process should state:

> Every employee has a right to a public hearing, peer evaluation, outside arbitration or some other open and mutually agreed upon grievance procedure before being demoted, unwillingly transferred, or fired.

Notice that while procedural due process gives employees the right to some form of open grievance procedure in which the employer is required to give *reasons* for his action, it does not require that the employer have *good* reasons. A second part of the right to due process would grant *substantive* guarantees that an employee cannot be fired or demoted without *good* reasons. Substantive due process will be discussed in Chapter Eight.

The right to due process in the workplace is an *issue* because it is not consistently protected by law. As recently as 1972 the Supreme Court ruled that a university that had dismissed a nontenured faculty member did not have to give reasons for that dismissal or provide the professor with any opportunity to question or appeal the decision.[5] Because of the lack of consistent legal recognition, one needs to justify the right to due process in private voluntary organizations on moral grounds.

First, respect for employees as persons would seem to require that an employer provide reasons for actions that affect employees. An employee cannot be expected to act autonomously if she cannot control or understand her employment. In particular, an action such as firing or demotion, which radically changes the future of an employee, calls for an explanation. This is not to say that most employers do not have reasons, even good reasons, for their actions. It is to require that these be stated openly and objectively to an employee and that she have some way to appeal or to respond.[6] Otherwise an employer is assuming that an employee does not deserve or will not be able to comprehend the rationale for demotion or firing. This surely shows a lack of respect for employees as persons since it denies them reasons for the treatment they receive, reasons that they as rational adults could comprehend.

Second, due process insures that an employer's decision will not be purely arbitrary, because the employer has to publicly justify her action. This, it seems to me, is valuable from an employer's perspective as well as from the point of view of an employee, for it makes public the poor judgments made by managers at all levels of employment, judgments that otherwise might not come to light.

Third, T. S. Scanlon claims that due process is "one of the conditions for the moral legitimacy of power-conferring institutions."[7] This is because due process morally restricts the conditions under which that power is used by requiring openness in decision-making. While Scanlon has in mind by and large public institutions, his statement applies to corporations as well. As we argued in Chapter Four, there is in most corporations an unequal distribution of power, such that those in positions having control of employment are in positions of relative power at least as that power relates to hiring and firing. Due process does not change this power hierarchy, but it is a means to check the possibility of arbitrary and therefore harmful misuses of that power, misuses that affect employees.

Finally, from a utilitarian perspective, as we argued at length in Chapter Four, arbitrary firing and demotion places employees at an unfair disadvantage vis-à-vis other employees or other persons seeking new em-

[5]*Board of Regents*. v. *Roth*, 408 U.S. (1972).

[6]Edmund L. Pincoffs, "Due Process, Fraternity, and a Kantian Injunction," in *Due Process*, J. Roland Pennock and John W. Chapman, eds. (New York: New York University Press, 1977), pp. 172–81.

[7]T. S. Scanlon, "Due Process," in Chapman and Pennock, p. 100.

ployment. It unduly harms employees who did not deserve to be fired because it is commonly assumed that persons who have been fired are incompetent, and gives other employees deserving to be fired or demoted equal status with those who do not. Such arbitrariness confers no benefit to productive organizations, save that it protects their alleged right to do as they please, a right surely restricted by whether or not exercising it harms other rights. Due process does not harm productive organizations since due process procedures need not be lengthy or interfere with efficient productivity. Well-organized procedures that evaluate the issue in question quickly as well as objectively do not slow business activity. In fact often internal due process procedures can avoid lengthy and costly court battles. Moreover, the practice of due process in the workplace can protect an employer against arbitrary actions by employees, since these procedures can be used to evaluate questionable *employee* activities that conflict with the goals of the organization.

Critics of the employee right to due process argue that even if it is true that EAW is to the advantage of the employer, the institution of due process in the workplace creates an imbalance of rights in favor of the employee, because it restricts the exercise of freedom of the employer without equally restricting the choices of the employee. Thus it merely replaces one unjust principle with another. But this objection is inaccurate. Due process does not alter employee-employer arrangements in place in an organization, nor does it infringe on an employer's prima facie right to dispose of production or what happens to that production. Due process does not require that employers never dismiss workers. It merely restricts the employer's alleged right to control employment without having to state reasons for particular employment decisions. This restriction improves rather than disturbs employee-employer relationships, because it strengthens mutual trust.

Second, due process appears to be an employee right that must be legally instituted and enforced. Such legal sanction adds to the coercive regulations currently forced on business. In response, however, it can be shown that due process procedures may be instituted voluntarily in the workplace. Many places of employment currently use various grievance procedures. (See the Appendix to this chapter for some illustrations.) Voluntarily instituting due process is one method to *prevent* further legislation.

A final criticism of due process in the workplace is that employees are sometimes afraid to use it because of fear of retaliation by a superior. Thus due process procedures are only window-dressings that do not really protect employees. Any so-called "open door" policy suffers in particular from such fears. This is a valid criticism, but it is scarcely a good reason for *not* instituting due process. Rather it suggests that there is a great need for very objective grievance policies in the workplace.

THE RIGHT TO FREEDOM IN THE WORKPLACE

Due process procedures call for employers publicly to justify their employment practices at least in firing and demoting. Part of the evaluation of employment practices is an assessment of whether employers respect the basic moral rights of their employees. One of these is the right to freedom. In the workplace this right is expressed in the rights to free expression and to bargain collectively and strike. These rights are challenged in at least two important circumstances: (a) when there is a conflict between an employee and the employer and the employee feels she needs to "blow the whistle" on the employer, and (b) when the rights to bargain collectively and to strike are curtailed.

In defending the right to free expression in the workplace there are two provisos. First, the right to freedom (and the corresponding right to blow the whistle) and the right to strike, are prima facie equal rights. Granting these in the workplace does not automatically grant license to speak out about everything or to strike on every occasion. Second, although free expression was an issue for George Geary and others, it is not true that employees have systematically been denied freedoms in the workplace. Rather, this usually becomes an issue only when there is a conflict between an employee and an employer concerning a moral or legal issue. When an exercise of freedom appears not to be in the interests of the employer, it is used as a reason to silence or fire the employee concerned or to prevent employees from striking. Yet these are the very instances when it would appear that employees need the right to freedom protected.

The Right to Free Expression and the Dilemmas of Whistle Blowers

Dan Gellert was, and still is, a pilot for Eastern Airlines. In 1972, when Gellert was involved in a flight training program for Eastern, he found a serious problem with the auto-pilot mechanism in the Lockheed 1011 aircraft that he and other pilots at Eastern were flying. He reported the defect first to a management official and later to the president, the chairman of the board of Eastern, and to Frank Borman, then vice-president of operations. Nothing was done. After the crash of an Eastern Airlines 1011 Gellert went to the National Transportation Safety Board (NTSB) where he testified about the problem. Still nothing was done to correct the auto-pilot. After a near-accident when flying the 1011 Gellert again went to the NTSB. Meanwhile Gellert was demoted to co-pilot and grounded although he had had twenty-five years flying experience and had served as a pilot trainer. Gellert then sued Eastern Airlines. During the litigation he was grounded two more times. Because of a strong pilot's union Gellert was not fired. He refused to quit because he felt that would ruin his reputation as a pilot, and because he knew he would be blackballed by other airlines. Gellert eventually won his law suit.

Five years later he is still with Eastern Airlines, and the auto-pilot mechanism on the Lockheed 1011 has been altered.[8]

Dan Gellert is a "whistle blower." Whistle-blowing in business occurs when an employee makes known or sounds an alarm either within the corporation or publicly about business activities he or she thinks will threaten individuals, the organization, or the public. It is a form of free speech prompted by circumstances that the whistle blower views as in some way morally or legally objectionable and that would probably go unnoticed otherwise. In this incident Dan Gellert was exercising his right to free expression, and he was exercising this right in a responsible manner. He did not wish to start trouble with his employer nor was he spreading malicious rumors about Eastern or Lockheed. Using what he thought were proper channels, Gellert was trying to call attention to an obvious danger in the Lockheed aircraft. Yet Gellert was "punished" for his actions.

The right to "blow the whistle" should be defined as the right not to be prevented from speaking out about illegal or immoral activities that occur in the workplace, and should include the right not to be harassed or punished when refusing to perform such objectionable activities.[9] Whistle-blowing, then, is an instantiation of a negative right (not to be coerced into silence) rather than a positive right (to say whatever one pleases at any time). Employees do not have the right to disclose confidential business information about their employer, for example, unless not disclosing that information would clearly harm the public. (More will be said about such disclosures later in the chapter.) Nor do employees have the right to slander other employees or their employer. On the other hand, if freedom is a basic moral right, employers do not have the right to restrict or "punish" legitimate whistle-blowing where a moral principle, an employee right, or the public interest is at stake.

Whistle-blowing activities take many forms. An employee may simply refuse to perform an action, a form of conscientious objection, or may protest within the company to his or her supervisor. Gellert began his protest by voicing his opinion within Eastern Airlines. Or the employee may, as Gellert did in the end, move to a public forum.

In all of these activities the whistle blower faces many dilemmas. First there is the question of evidence. The whistle blower must be sure of her facts, she must have good reasons to support her evidence, and she must be

---

[8]Dan Gellert, "Whistle Blower: Dan Gellert, Airline Pilot," *The Civil Liberties Review*, September–October 1978, rpt. in *Individual Rights in the Corporation*, Alan F. Westin and Stephan Salisbury, eds. (New York: Pantheon Books, 1980), pp. 106–10.

[9]For discussions of whistle-blowing, see Tom Donaldson, *Corporations and Morality* (Englewood Cliffs: Prentice-Hall, Inc., 1982), pp. 144–49, and Norman Bowie, *Business Ethics* (Englewood Cliffs, N.J.: Prentice-Hall, Inc., 1982), pp. 138–48.

able to document the case. In blowing the whistle an employee is calling into question the accountability relationship between herself and her employer. Such a breach of loyalty must be justifiable. The whistle blower is arguing that an overriding moral or professional commitment outweighs her role loyalty and responsibilities as an employee. In some cases if the danger is to a third party, such as the danger to the customer in Geary's case, one is torn between the responsibility to expose the danger and the knowledge that the exposure could damage one's company. In other cases, professional loyalties cause conflicts of interest. The employees at Goodrich Corporation who finally went to the FBI about the faulty brake faced these sorts of dilemmas. In whistle-blowing, then, there often occurs a conflict of responsibilities, one's role in a company and loyalty to one's job in contrast to professional commitments and to what appears to be the morally correct course.

Whistle blowers often have to make moral choices between ideals that are of conflicting but equal weight. In evaluating the whistle-blowing activity, a potential whistle blower must weigh not only the harm created by the questionable activity and the possible benefits to be accrued from blowing the whistle, but also the possible harm that blowing the whistle might cause. The whistle blower knows that her action will disrupt the workplace and, in turn, might endanger the jobs of other employees. Every whistle blower feels a conflict between whistle blowing and loyalties to her family. Most whistle blowers lose their jobs, and many are "blackballed" from related jobs in the industry. Consequently the whistle blower must employ utilitarian tests as well as moral principles in evaluating the action, because she must be convinced that the issue, if not resolved, will cause real harm that would otherwise go unresolved.

From the employer's point of view, whistle-blowing is, at best, a disquieting occurrence in the workplace. As we saw earlier, International Harvester fired Ray Palmateer even though he helped local police track down employee theft at International Harvester. Harvester argued that this was an internal matter best handled within the company. What they were objecting to was an act of public whistle blowing that disrupted the normal business of Harvester. They feared that Palmateer, like some whistle blowers they had heard about, would continue to be a troublemaker at the plant. Employees, too, do not always welcome whistle-blowing, because it disrupts the workplace and creates employer distrust of other employees. But these objections do not *justify* firing whistle blowers such as Palmateer unless the whistle blower has no basis for her action. This is because firing legitimate whistle blowers is a denial of free speech and questions the exercise of that right in the workplace, thus questioning its exercise elsewhere. But from an employer's point of view these objections help to explain why whistle blowing is not a popular employee practice in the workplace.

Finally, whistle-blowing may not always be the best thing to do, all things considered. Sometimes simply to blow the whistle when a wrong is committed is neither the most responsible course of action nor does it achieve the desired result. In some cases one can stay at one's job, abstain from whistle-blowing, and resolve the problem in question.

This discussion is not meant to underestimate the value of free expression and whistle-blowing in the workplace. Had Gellert not spoken out the automechanism in the Lockheed airplane would in all likelihood have gone unrepaired until some serious accident occurred. But we should be reminded that the right to free expression is a prima facie negative right. Because whistle-blowing challenges employer rights and whistle blowers face unpleasant and difficult choices, it is not an action to be considered lightly. At the same time, the exercise of legitimate whistle-blowing, as a substantive right to free expression, needs to be protected from employer retaliation.

The Right to Bargain Collectively and the Right to Strike

Although many political rights cannot be exercised in the workplace without danger of employer retaliation, most employees have in the last twenty years acquired the freedom to bargain collectively for employee wants and have also enjoyed the right to strike. Traditionally these rights are thought of as economic as well as political rights because they balance employer economic control over employees. These are functions that are justified because they equalize the unfair advantage that the employer has by reason of the control of employment opportunities, wages, job benefits, and property rights that result from private ownership. The right to bargain collectively gives employees the power to balance employer economic authority with collective employee strength. The right to strike recognizes that employees have economic options to stop work if their legitimate demands are not honored in the workplace. Like the right to bargain collectively, the right to strike balances the employer's contention that it should be able to offer jobs, wages, and benefits at will.

All employees in the public and private sector enjoy the right to bargain collectively. However the 1981 strike by air controllers illustrates that not all public employees enjoy the right to strike, a right that is often the only avenue of employee protest. To deny the right to strike to certain groups of employees, such as those in the public sector of the economy, is unfair because these employees do not receive the same consideration as employees in the private sector who *can* strike. The denial of this right places them at a disadvantage in relation to their employer. It means that they must acquiesce to employer demands, however unjust, or leave their jobs, while employees in the private sector of the economy can often strike under similar circumstances. This is not to suggest that the city, state, and federal government employers who hire civil servants treat them unfairly. By and large these employers are very fair. The issue, like others in this book, is a question of rights. Why should civil employees have to depend on the benevolence of their employers without any balancing powers of redress? Why should the employee-employer relationship rest on the ultimate right of the employer to exercise his prerogative against employee strikes? And what is to protect the civil employee against the injustices that do occur? Without the right to strike these groups of employees have no economic weapons to protest low salaries, the lack of benefits, poor working conditions, or the absence of employee rights in the workplace.

The justification for denying the right to strike to public sector employees is that public welfare is an overriding concern. Strikes by public employees such as air controllers or postal workers would not be in the national interest, and indeed would do serious damage to the national welfare. However this justification is erroneous for it could be used equally well to argue that *any* right to strike is not in the national interest. For example, a strike by the Teamsters is much more damaging than a strike by air controllers simply by virtue of the important elements of national transportation for which the Teamsters are responsible. Yet it would be difficult to maintain that the Teamsters should be prohibited from striking, because such a denial would give employers an unfair advantage over Teamster workers. Interestingly most hospital workers, who deal with life-threatening activities, have the right to strike, while persons in less sensitive but public activities do not have such a right. Thus if employees have the right to strike, which, as a balance or economic redress, they do, then all employees in every sector of the economy should enjoy this right as well. The right to strike is a prima facie right because in times of national emergency, for example when one's right to life is in danger, the right to strike is usually overridden by the right to survival. But public interests, like economic interests, cannot be used as justification for overriding the right to strike unless there is the threat of a greater harm to *rights*. In most instances this is not the case.

Striking is commonly justified as an activity that balances employer economic control. In the case of public employees it might be used to balance the government's coercive or unfair treatment of civil servants. While it has traditionally been used as a weapon to improve wages and working conditions, it *could* be used politically to redress other employee rights grievances. For example, had the salespersons at U.S. Steel struck collectively in defense of George Geary, the outcome might have been different. If employees have rights in the workplace, they also have obligations to protest the abrogation of those rights through collective bargaining and walkouts. Striking for no justified reason is, of course, illegitimate and strikers who do so deserve employer or governmental retaliation.

FREEDOM AND PRIVACY

The right to freedom is related to the right to privacy. Privacy protects personal freedom and autonomy by keeping personal and intimate information in the hands of its rightful "owner." It is, in fact, a necessary condition for autonomy. It is a violation of freedom to destroy privacy by permitting access to, and the possible control of, information persons wish to keep to themselves. Free expression is a basic moral right, which, as we argued in Chapter Four, cannot be set aside for economic interests, even when these interests benefit those whose rights are being violated. Similarly, we shall argue that the right to privacy is another important basic moral right of employees.

THE RIGHT TO PRIVACY IN THE WORKPLACE

In a recent incident an employee-run Credit Union of a major corporation was faced with a conflict between their own financial interests and the rights of an employee-member. The employee wished to take out a loan with the Credit Union to buy a car. Although the employee's credit references were not negative, the Credit Union manager knew that this employee had had trouble paying his bills. The employee had changed addresses several times and was a bad credit risk. Unfortunately the Credit Union's knowledge of the employee's background was based on confidential information supposedly known only to the personnel office. Therefore the Credit Union manager felt she had to lend money to the employee, even though the loan jeopardized the Credit Union since, in safeguarding the employee's privacy she had no *right* to the information she had learned.[10]

The right to privacy includes, but is not defined merely as, (1) the right to be left alone (that is, the negative right to freedom), (2) the related right to autonomy,[11] and (3) "the claim of individuals, groups, or institutions to determine for themselves when, how, and to what extent information about them is communicated to others."[12] Why are these three kinds of privacy such important rights? As a rational adult one has the right to autonomy: the right to make choices and to direct one's own life so long as these choices do not affect the freedom of others. If one has the right to choose for oneself, one also has the right to protect oneself from outside interference. If personhood is individual, I have a right to isolate myself

[10]Told to me privately by the personnel officer of the corporation. Name withheld at the request of the company.

[11]Elizabeth L. Beardsley, "Privacy: Autonomy and Selective Disclosure," in *Privacy: Nomos 13*, J. Roland Pennock and John W. Chapman, eds. (New York: Atherton Press, Inc., 1971), pp. 56–70.

[12]Alan Westin, *Privacy and Freedom* (New York: Atheneum Press, 1967), p. 7.

from the invasion of others. Thus I am entitled to control what others know about me as a person and what information about myself will be disseminated. Unless their privacy is respected persons lose a sense of self-identity, because what separates one from another, what identifies her to herself, becomes indistinguishable from what others know about her. Without privacy one's personal freedom is, at best, restricted, since the source of free choice, one's autonomy, is not safeguarded.

Moreover, respect for privacy safeguards the misuse of personal information. In the case cited above, the privacy of the potential loan customer could not be disregarded even though it was in the economic interests of the company to reveal confidential information about the person. Such privacy violations would set precedents for future violations of privacy in other situations, as for example when an employer might wish to know about the political activities or the voting record of an employee.

In the workplace the right to privacy includes at least four activities. First, the employee has a right to limit access to information he or she gives to an employer. In no case should this information be given to any outside person or organization without the express permission of the employee. This is because an employer's *right* to personal information is coupled with an obligation to safeguard that data. Otherwise the employer threatens the autonomy of the employee by making his or her personal life a subject for unwarranted scrutiny.

Second, despite the wishes of employers such as Sheriff Elrod, cited in the introduction to Part Two, an employee has a right to activities of his or her choice outside the workplace. Otherwise the employee is literally part of the corporation and cannot have an independent life. Such dependence is tantamount to slavery.

Third, *employers* have the right to the privacy of business information so long as this information does not threaten public welfare. Confidential business information belongs to the employer just as personal information belongs to the employee. Revealing such information might be as harmful to an employer as unnecessary disclosure of personnel information is harmful to an employee. This is because the disclosure of confidential business affairs restricts the employer's ability to act freely and to control the organization's business activities.

Fourth, the employee has a right to privacy of thought, a right brought into question of late by the use of polygraphs or lie detectors. We will discuss this right in detail in the next section.

A businessperson might object to these exaggerated claims for the right to privacy, particularly as this right functions in the workplace. Strict confidentiality and employee privacy must sometimes be sacrificed for an employer's business freedom and to protect other employees and consumers. Moreover, businesses are often held liable for employee actions when these actions are connected with their employment and are therefore obligated to retain safe and competent employees.[13] Information on employees or prospective employees, including on occasion polygraph information, is necessary to protect the employer against possible employee actions that would incriminate the business and sometimes to protect honest and innocent employees against wrongful incrimination. We will respond to these objections in the discussion of the polygraph.

The Polygraph and Privacy

The right to privacy is brought into serious question by the prolific use of the polygraph in employment. The polygraph is employed in every area of the workplace from local taverns (to make sure bartenders are turning in all the cash they receive) to department stores (where employees are routinely checked for stolen merchandise or money). Because the polygraph explores one's most private thoughts its use, I shall argue, violates rights to privacy more than surveillance or the publicizing of confidential records. The polygraph, I shall argue, violates the right to privacy of both honest *and* dishonest employees to such an extent that economic interests never justify its use.

Objections to the Polygraph

The use of the polygraph is a clear case of conflict between employer rights and employee rights to autonomy and freedom. Can the right to freedom and personal privacy be set aside when an employer's productive activities are threatened? What rights does an employer have to protect his or her property and well-being?

No person has rights to the thoughts and feelings of another person. The polygraph invades a bastion of privacy unique to persons—the self. Without the privacy of our thoughts our autonomy as individuals is forfeited. The polygraph allows very personal information to get into the hands of others. Employers seldom misuse this information, but if the right to the most private elements of one's personality can be overridden to protect employer or even employee economic interests, then the right to privacy could be overridden to protect other collective interests as well, for example society's interest in knowing who has dissident political thoughts or who engages in socially questionable but harmless activities. Thus the existence of the lie detector threatens very basic political rights because it allows economic interests or collective welfare to violate freedom and privacy.

---

[13]See John C. North, "The Responsibility of Employers for the Actions of their Employees: The Negligent Hiring Theory of Liability," *Chicago-Kent Law Review*, 53 (1977), pp. 717–30.

On a practical level there are many problems with the use of the polygraph. First, while taking a lie detector test is voluntary according to the law, a refusal to take the test is often interpreted by an employer as a sign of guilt. Therefore the "voluntariness" of the test is questionable, at best. Second, there is the practical problem of test accuracy. The test is accurate between 65% and 90% of the time. Let us suppose the test is 90% accurate. This means that if one tests 100 employees and 10 out of that 100 are found guilty according to the polygraph results, at least one out of the ten found guilty is really innocent under the best of testing conditions. In order to find the guilty party or parties one has to sacrifice the innocence of one person. No test is worth the loss of one person's freedom, particularly when the inaccuracies of testing are such that up to 35% of the persons found guilty by the polygraph may in reality be innocent.[14] There is also a difficulty with the nature of the questions asked by the polygraph tester. Although they are supposed to be factual in content, many of them arouse such deep emotions in the testee that they trigger guilt-like reactions on the lie detector. On the other hand persons familiar with the lie detector contend that they can pass *any* polygraph test.

Suppose one could so devise a polygraph and train those who administer the tests that the test was 100% accurate. This would answer the practical objections to the examination, but even the perfect polygraph fails the test of preserving moral rights. It drastically reduces human privacy, and it fails the requirement of universality since one would not want the polygraph to be employed everywhere in all instances. Managers, for instance, would complain if they were always subject to polygraph examinations in conjunction with employee tests. Therefore since the polygraph threatens very basic human rights, its abolishment should be seriously considered.

If one outlaws the polygraph what should an employer do when there is excessive employee theft? Employers do have the right to protect their business, and practical means other than the polygraph are available that safeguard property without threatening rights. Dismissal with hearing and prosecution of employees proven guilty are, for example, very effective ways to deter employee misbehavior. Many companies dismiss employees caught stealing, but seldom does any company prosecute guilty employees. Sometimes they are even given bland letters of recommendation! This employer inertia simply encourages more employee theft. Employers need to be creative in tracking down and preventing employee criminality, but they need to do so without violating rights.

---

[14]See George Brenkert, "Corporations, Polygraphs and Privacy," *Journal of Business and Professional Ethics,* 1 (1981), pp. 19–36.

CONCLUSION

The rights to due process and freedom are moral rights recognized legally by the Constitution. To deny due process in the workplace is inconsistent with the principles of a democratic society committed to the exercise of universal fair treatment. Freedom and privacy are basic moral rights, the legitimate exercise of which cannot be used as a reason for dismissal or demotion without questioning the universality of these as *rights*. These rights extend the notion of due process as merely a formal procedure in the workplace by disallowing legitimate whistle-blowing, striking, and demands for personal privacy as substantive grounds or "good reasons" for firing and demotion. But all we have established from a moral point of view is that due process should be instituted in the workplace, and that freedom and privacy should be respected there. Should these rights be legally protected as well? The ideal, of course, would be the voluntary extension of all constitutionally guaranteed rights to the workplace along with the right to privacy and the right to strike. This need not be either difficult or expensive, as we pointed out in the analysis of the right to due process. In the appendix to this chapter some specific policies for implementing the rights to due process, freedom, and privacy are spelled out. These are models for voluntary employer compliance. But the question is, will this voluntarism occur in the workplace? If it does not then the legal institution of employee rights is both justified and necessary.

APPENDIX

Specific Programs

**POLICIES FOR THE
INSTITUTION OF DUE PROCESS
IN THE WORKPLACE**

Despite problems with due process, a number of companies employ a variety of grievance procedures with success. Many have written grievance policies that are publicly distributed to all employees. At some corporations, such as McDonald's and General Electric, an ombudsman acts as an objective buffer between workers and management. At the Northrup Corporation there are three steps of appeal: there is an ombudsman for the first appeal; there is a three-member arbitration board that hears all employee complaints; and in severe cases outside arbitrators are hired to settle the dispute. Any employee can select a co-worker to help in the defense or to act on one of the boards of arbitrators.

In outline, due process in the workplace should include the following:

1. Written contracts between employees and employers should be drawn up at the time of hiring in which the rights and responsibilities of each party are spelled out.
2. Written due process policies should be drawn up and made public to all employees.
3. "Open Door" policies of employee complaints should be instituted stipulating that complaints are truly welcomed and will be promptly resolved. An anonymous complaint procedure is very effective. An ombudsman or an employee advocate is helpful because employees have fewer fears of retaliation if there are designated persons available for such purposes.
4. Any employee who has an unanswered complaint against an employer or who feels he or she has been demoted or fired without good reason

should have the right to appeal through a formal set of procedures.

5. Employees should be protected from employer retaliation against employees who use the due process procedure as a form of grievance or appeal.

Formal Procedures

6.   a. Formal appeals should begin with a written complaint, where possible.

b. The complainant should appoint an employee advocate or co-worker to attend each hearing.

c. The complaint should be heard first by one's immediate supervisor, next by a department head.

7. A peer review committee to review complaints not settled with the above procedures should be formulated.

8. An appeals committee consisting of representatives from management, from the peer committee, and a co-worker should review the decision of the peer committee.

9. If all the foregoing fail and the employee persists in her or his grievance, outside arbitrators should be brought in to evaluate the decision.

10. All parts of this process should be open and prompt.

11. Any person unjustly demoted or fired should be reinstated with back pay and/or equal compensation.

Employer Rights

12. Any employer who has a complaint against an employee should similarly go through these formal procedures.

13. Any employee found guilty as charged should be demoted or fired without penalty to the employer.

POLICIES FOR THE INSTITUTION OF FREEDOM IN THE WORKPLACE

Free Expression and Whistle-Blowing

1. Any employee has the right to speak out in protest of a product, employee treatment or other organizational activity on legal or moral grounds, without risk of reprimand or job loss. The objectionable activity may be in the public interest, e.g., nuclear plant activities, or a private but moral concern, e.g., employee mistreatment. The form of free expression may be through such means as a company suggestion box or speaking to a superior. (At Dow Chemical Company and American Airlines a company newspaper is provided to air complaints and grievances.[1])

2. The whistle blower or conscientious objector is to be protected initially from employer retaliation.

[1]See David Ewing, "Employee Freedom Within the Organization," *Proceedings of the Second National Conference on Business Ethics,* Michael Hoffman, ed., (Washington, D.C.: University Press of America, 1979), p. 171.

3. The whistle blower is expected to document the charge. If this is not achieved, the matter should be dropped. Documentation may be achieved through (a) written proof, (b) examination by employee-employer committees, and/or (c) outside expert evaluation.
4. Documented cases that are ignored, or are likely to be ignored, should be aired to a professional organization or through a public medium. If the charges are true, the employee blowing the whistle should be protected by statute from employer retaliation or discrimination.
5. Slanderous or clearly false accusations by whistle blowers should result in the dismissal of the employee making such charges and, when appropriate, legal punishment.

It has also been suggested that anonymous whistle-blowing should be encouraged to protect employees from employer retaliation.[2] The problem with this sort of activity is that often the whistle blower is suspected or known. Such knowledge often damages employee-employer relationships more seriously than public recognition of the whistle blower. Further, anonymous whistle blowing encourages slanderous or unfair accusations that damage the employer and impair the encouragement of legitimate whistle blowing. Adequate protection of whistle blowing makes anonymity unnecessary.

Protecting The Right to Strike

1. Every employee has the right to bargain collectively.
2. Every employee has the right to strike.
3. It is the responsibility of the strikers to demonstrate that their claims are justified.
4. If a strike is unwarranted, strikers may lose their jobs and/or be subject to legitimate legal punishment. The right to bargain collectively and the right to strike are important as two guarantees for the recognition of employee demands.

PROGRAMS FOR THE PROTECTION OF PRIVACY IN THE WORKPLACE

The constitutional right to privacy is not always protected in the workplace. There are often good reasons for this when employer rights are threatened by employee invasions, but sometimes employers unthinkingly do not protect confidential employee information. Sometimes employers restrict outside activities of employees. And the polygraph is a standard method of employee behavior control. The solution to protecting the right to privacy of employees which should not threaten employer rights, I would suggest, is the following program.

[2]Fredrick Elliston, "Anonymous Whistle Blowing," *Business and Professional Ethics*, 1 (1982), pp. 39–58.

1. The Privacy Act should be adopted for all employees in the public and private sector. This act protects employees from undue disclosures and surveillance.

2. The polygraph should be outlawed. Its invasion of the rights to privacy and freedom overrides any value such a test might have even for hardened criminals, and its inaccuracies do not validate any utilitarian justification.

3. Employees proven guilty of theft or other employer property damage should be dismissed and brought before the law. Such persons harm the property of employers and of employees. They give a bad name to trustworthy employees, and their example encourages employers to engage in repressive treatment of employees such as the use of the polygraph.

4. Employees who reveal confidential business information should be dismissed. Employees who have left the company should be prosecuted.

5. Employer-Employee Committees should be set up to:
    a. evaluate the protection or dissemination of confidential information, including employee personal information and employer business information.
    b. resolve questions of privacy that might occur in employee-employer relationships.
    c. draw up written policies stating employee and employer privacy rights.

6. Any so-called necessary violation of the rights to employee privacy, say for security interests, should be announced publicly, such procedures should be evaluated by the Employee-Employer Committee before being instituted, and the procedures for such violations should be made public to the employees.

7. Any employer policies restricting employee outside activities should be made public and stated in writing to all prospective and current employees. And any such restriction should be evaluated by the Employee-Employer Committee, which should have the final decision as to the implementation of such a policy. In general such restrictions would appear to violate important rights to privacy and to freedom except in times of national emergencies.

7

Economic Rights in the Workplace: Safety, Fair Pay, Participation, and Meaningful Work

Are these men and women
Workers of the world?
or is it an overgrown nursery
with children—goosing, slapping, boys
giggling, snotty girls?
What is it about that entrance way,
those gates to the plant? Is it the
guards, the showing of your badge—the smell?
is there some invisible eye
that pierces you through and
transforms your being? Some aura
of ether, that brain and spirit washes you
and commands, "For eight hours
you shall be different."
What is it that instantaneously makes
a child out of a man?
Moments before he was a father, a husband,
an owner of property,
a voter, a lover, an adult.
When he spoke at least some listened.
Salesmen courted his favor.
Insurance men appealed to his family responsibility
and by chance the church sought his help. . . .

But that was before he shuffled past the guard,
climbed the steps,
hung up his coat and
took his place along the line.[1]

Granting political rights in the workplace is necessary in any society that espouses these rights. However, even when political rights are recognized in the workplace, this alone does not assure that the workplace will be safe, happy, or productive. Employee rights encompass important economic entitlements as well. These are often called economic rights, since they are claims peculiar to economic activities. Some derive from the basic moral rights that we discussed in the Introduction to the book. These economic rights are as important as the political rights to due process, to freedom, and to privacy, and some of them, too, are not always honored in the workplace. Economic rights that are most closely derived from basic moral rights include, but are not limited to, the right to a safe workplace, the right to fair pay, and the right to participation. Together their aim is to make work not merely politically fair but also meaningful to employees.

In the climate of new interest in employee rights that characterizes the 1980s, many persons have suggested that workers have a right to participate in decision-making processes, in management, and/or on the board of directors of their company. It is argued that participation of every worker and worker self-management are essential for worker freedom and self-development. Persons who hold this position are concerned that required menial tasks—or any tasks done at the request of a superior—are restrictions on freedom.[2] A radical version of this view questions the traditional capitalist hierarchical structure in corporations as necessarily destructive to positive human freedom.

This extreme position may overstate the excesses of free enterprise. Although participation in the workplace may add to the job satisfaction of many workers, this is not true in all cases. To force persons into management positions may neither be in their best interest nor enhance their job satisfaction. Rather, persons should have the real opportunity to participate in the workplace, but not a binding obligation to do so. Those who truly do not want to become involved in management should not be so forced. Management-employee relationships are not necessarily destructive of worker self-development if employee rights are recognized, if there is a respectful reciprocity in employee-management relationships, and if

[1]Quoted in Thomas J. Peters and Robert H. Waterman, Jr., *In Search of Excellence* (New York: Harper & Row, Publishers, 1982), pp. 235–36. The poem was allegedly written for an auto workers' underground paper at General Motors. Reprinted by permission of the publisher.

[2]See especially Adina Schwartz, "Meaningful Work," *Ethics*, 92 (1982), pp. 634–46, and "Autonomy in the Workplace," in *Just Business*, Tom Regan ed. (New York: Random House, 1984), pp. 129–65.

those in management positions truly allow participation by interested workers. In what follows I shall argue that participation and participatory management are very important for the exercise of autonomy and positive freedom. "Flattening management hierarchy," about which we shall speak more later, is not antithetical to capitalism, but enforced participation and egalitarianism in the workplace are as restrictive on employee freedoms as the allegedly coercive hierarchy they are to replace.

A major objective of any participatory management program is to make work meaningful for employees. Two conditions are necessary, however, to guarantee the minimally decent working conditions that foster this objective: fair pay and a safe workplace. Before discussing participation in the workplace, let us examine these conditions.

FAIR PAY

One of the conditions for the acceptability of a job, not to mention its significance, is that one be paid fairly for one's contribution. At a minimum, fair pay includes (a) on the basis of equal consideration, the right to receive equal pay for equal work in comparison to other workers in similar jobs, and (b) on the basis of the right to subsistence, the right to be paid at least subsistence wages for one's work. The latter is based on the idea that if one has the right to life, to subsistence and to freedom, one has the right to do as one pleases including working in order to live. If one works, one contributes something, productivity, and one has a right to something in exchange. If one has a full-time job, one is trading *all* of one's productivity, and thus one has a right to at least a subsistence wage for that exchange. Otherwise the trade is in violation of the rights to life and to subsistence. These two conditions, however, equal pay for equal work and subsistence wages, only establish the necessary conditions for fair pay. Sufficient conditions are more difficult to determine. Does fair pay *always* mean equal pay, or can one justify differences in income for different tasks?

In a capitalist economy a number of factors contribute to determining one's pay. These include the market value of the job, the scarcity of workers for that type of task, the possible dangers of the position, job responsibilities, the power of the position, and the value of its contribution to the needs and interests of society. Sometimes factors such as the popularity or marketability of a job or a talent contribute heavily to determining one's income. This is true, for example, in the case of good athletes. One will debate endlessly which of these factors is the most fair and which is the least fair. Is it fair, for example, to pay Wilt Chamberlain so much for his abilities in basketball? Is it right that the president of General Motors makes a larger salary than the president of the United States? Should the discoverer of polio vaccine receive less income than the inventor of the instant camera? We cannot settle this debate to everyone's satisfaction. But we can suggest two principles of fairness that might be used as tools to evaluate differences in remuneration.

First, as we noted earlier, Henry Shue in his book *Basic Rights* argues that everyone has the right to subsistence. He claims further that this right is so basic and universal that when it is not realized those who have wealth should be required to give up some of it in order to provide subsistence for others. One criterion for judging inequalities in remuneration, then, is whether everyone in a particular society has their basic needs satisfied. If they do not, then pay differentials are unjust until everyone has at least a subsistence income. In our society this is taken care of, albeit inadequately, by taxation of incomes and transfer payments to the poor.

A second way to evaluate inequalities in pay is to appeal to John Rawls' famous difference principle. About this principle Rawls says:

> All social primary goods—liberty and opportunity, income and wealth, and the bases of self-respect—are to be distributed equally unless an unequal distribution of any or all of these goods is to the advantage of the least favored.[3]

Inequalities in pay, then, are justified only if they benefit everyone and are to the disadvantage of no one.

According to this view unequal pay is justified when:

a. a job is exceedingly dangerous and societally necessary. (Climbing Mount Everest would not qualify.)

b. incentives are needed to increase the number of workers or professionals in a certain field.

c. the position or the person in the position makes a marked and positive contribution to society, and/or the absence of that position or that person would create marked suffering to a society.

d. the responsibilities of the job are greater than for most jobs, and there are few who can or are willing to master that responsibility.

e. the unequal pay or income does not create a situation which allows those paid more than others to be in an advantageous economic position of power as a result of that income, such that that power is to the unfair disadvantage, or negatively affects the rights and privileges of others in that society.

In our society, as the foregoing examples of pay differences illustrate, there are no consistent principles or guidelines for fair pay. What is needed is an examination of remuneration and pay scales with regard to Shue's

---

[3]This statement is derived from his famous Difference Principle which states, "Social and economic inequalities are to be arranged so that they are both (a) to the greatest benefit to the least advantaged . . . [and] (b) attached to offices and positions open to all under conditions of fair equality of opportunity." John Rawls, *A Theory of Justice* (Cambridge: Harvard University Press, 1971), pp. 302–3.

subsistence proviso and with Rawls' difference principle in mind. Unfair disadvantages that result from unjustified inequalities in pay can and should be eliminated.

THE RIGHT TO A SAFE WORKPLACE

Despite advances in the technology of work, the safety of workers in this country is still an important problem. We have successfully and safely put persons on the moon, but we have not paid sufficient attention to developing technology to provide a safe workplace for all our employees. Every year thousands of persons are disabled by black lung disease from coal mining, brown lung disease from working in cotton mills, asbestos poisoning, prolonged exposure to dangerous chemicals of various sorts, and other working dangers.

There are a number of reasons why not all places of work are safe.

1. Employers are sometimes negligent. They have knowledge of, or can inform themselves about work risks, but they fail to do so, fail to inform their employees, and neglect to reduce known risks. Few employers, however, are calculably disinterested in worker safety. More than likely work hazards exist for other reasons, such as the following.

2. It is often too expensive to improve plant safety without putting the employer out of business. One could, for example remove all the risks from driving an automobile, but then no one could afford to own a car. Similarly, even if it were technically feasible to make the workplace risk free, this would be impossible from an economic point of view.

3. There is a paucity of information about many work hazards. It may be that both employees and employers lack such information, and sometimes neither party tries to inform themselves adequately of work hazards. It may be that employers are not sufficiently informed concerning the nature and scope of the risks in a particular occupation, or that, if they are so informed, they do not pass on this information to their employees.

4. Some occupations are inherently dangerous. For example, despite the latest technology coal mining is a dangerous occupation. Black lung disease is only partially preventable even in the most modern mines.

5. Some workers simply accept dangers as part of the job. And some, such as coal miners, have difficulty finding safe jobs for which they are qualified.

6. Some employees do not practice care and create work dangers.

7. Safety in the workplace is not a top priority of research and technology.

None of these factors *excuses* the neglect of worker safety, but they point to complexities in what at first appears to be a simple matter of instituting safety in the workplace.

The issue of worker safety is a three-fold problem. First, what *rights* has the worker to safe working conditions? What rights has the employer? Second, is the *recognition* of these rights enough to guarantee a safe workplace? And third, how can working conditions be practically improved to the satisfaction of the employee without making excessive financial demands on the employer?

That workers have a right to safety in the workplace might seem too obvious to argue. Yet because safety is not a priority in all companies, it is worth outlining the foundations for that right. Dangerous working conditions violate moral rights, rights so basic that we have scarcely discussed them in this essay: the rights to life and to survival. These rights are so important that if persons do not have them, the other rights we have defended in this book are of little value. Dangerous conditions that threaten life or health threaten the very survival of persons. Dangerous working conditions threaten the very existence of employees and cannot be countenanced when they are avoidable. The right to due process in the workplace, upon which we placed such emphasis, loses its significance for workers whose psychological health or physical well-being are threatened by work hazards.

Second, workers (as well as employers) have a right to information about work hazards, just as they have rights to other business information pertinent to their employment and future. This knowledge should include information about the probability of the risk, its magnitude, and the short-term and long-term consequences for one's health. Employers have an obligation to investigate possible work risks so that they can inform workers and seek remedies for employment dangers. Lack of information makes intelligent choices about accepting or refusing work impossible, thus reducing employees' ability to function as intelligent adults. Until recently, for example, few employees were fully informed about the dangers of working with asbestos although there is a great deal of evidence to suggest that information about its dangers was readily available in the 1930s, information that companies such as Manville either did not seek or ignored, and which, in any case, was not relayed to their employees.[4] Thus these workers could not make informed choices as to whether or not to continue to work with asbestos. In such cases it is not unjustified to put full blame for subsequent worker illnesses and disabilities on the employer, since employees were kept ignorant of the issue and thus are not at all culpable.

Third, respect for workers as persons requires that workers should have the right to conscientious objection when they do not wish to accept a hazardous job. This is properly called "informed refusal" since a worker needs to be informed about the work hazard before she can decide freely whether or not to accept the assignment.

The right to a safe workplace, the right to information, and the right to informed refusal are vague claims unless one sets criteria for what would count as a safe workplace and what would count as adequate information.

---

[4]Jeff Coplon, "Left in the Dust," *Village Voice*, March 1, 1983, pp. 1–34.

In each particular manufacturing context these criteria will be different. In general, however, the ideal for safety would be a place in which preventable hazards are alleviated to the maximum extent possible given the financial conditions of the business. Criteria for the "maximum extent possible" could be judged by what is called the "reasonable or professional person" standard, criteria a well-informed person would adopt in an ideal business situation. It would remain the burden of the employer to inform employees about remaining work hazards, explain why certain ideal conditions are not met, and allow informed conscientious objection.

Providing information about work hazards and allowing informed refusal in the workplace do not necessarily protect the worker who accepts dangers in employment as a matter of course. There are two remedies for worker disinterest or management apathy. First, workers should have the opportunity, and indeed the obligation, to participate in making decisions and policies that affect their safety. Second, unlike most employee rights for which this book has argued, worker safety needs to be protected by law to reinforce employer and employee concerns, and to override employer and employee apathy. Employees should be required to develop and adopt safety measures to protect themselves and fellow employees. Employers should be economically encouraged to adopt safety regulations in the workplace through tax benefits and reduction of workers' compensation payments for safe plants.

PARTICIPATION IN THE WORKPLACE

Worker safety and fair pay are necessary for decent working conditions. Many thinkers argue that they are also *sufficient* to provide the proper economic climate for worker satisfaction. Anything more infringes on employer rights and threatens the efficiency, productivity, and profitability without which there would be no jobs, and thus no employee rights to protect. Some of these arguments were criticized in earlier chapters. In the following sections we shall make the more positive statement that involving employees in their work through information, worker participation programs, and other forms of work enhancement increases workers' interest in their jobs, makes working more significant to them, and produces a more loyal and productive work force. From a less utilitarian perspective, such worker involvement is consistent with the theory of basic rights, since the right to participation is an instantiation of the basic moral right to autonomy and self-development. From the perspective of the reciprocity of employee-employer relationships, if productivity is a contribution to the corporation, then it is only consistent to argue that in return for this, every effort should be made to make working meaningful to the employee.

Meaningful Work

Ever since Karl Marx wrote about the alienation of labor in the nineteenth century, theorists and business persons have been concerned to make jobs meaningful to employees. But what does the term "meaningful" signify? A meaningful job is one the employee enjoys and excels in, feeling himself in control of the work activity. Meaningful work requires that one have information about one's job, one's future at that job, and the future of the business. Otherwise job decisions are not informed ones. Since work enjoyment can develop from involvement in business decisions, meaningful employment often requires participation in the decision-making processes in the workplace. This participation could be as slight as choosing one's work hours or it could include taking responsibility as part of a team for the manufacture of a certain product. Participation might also extend to full participation in the management and the decisions of the business.[5] In its most radical interpretation, meaningful work is equated with worker control and/or ownership of the means of production as Marx proposed.

However, since each of us perceives what is important and meaningful at work from a different perspective, the concept of meaningful work cannot be merely identified with participation or defined in terms of participatory management. This is because despite the fact that repetitive or menial tasks are usually thought of as dull and degrading, some persons—though probably very few—are not dissatisfied with such work. There are even those, working to their capacities, for whom so-called menial tasks are neither dull nor degrading.[6] Other persons identify meaningful work with a certain position, a title, or with remuneration. Still others, such as researchers, define a meaningful job as one where they are left alone. Taking any part in management or participatory decision-making is, for these persons, contrary to their notion of work satisfaction.

In all definitions of meaningful work there is included a need for a sense of satisfaction (albeit different in each case), an identity with the work as "my job," and most importantly the notion that the employee can freely choose or be offered job alternatives and/or the opportunity, but not the obligation, to participation in ways that are meaningful to her. Without some identity or satisfaction with a job, one feels no sense of loyalty or commitment. The work is of no consequence.

Participation and the Right to a Meaningful Job

The right to a meaningful job is an instantiation of the positive right to freedom, because it acknowledges the autonomy, independence, and

---

[5]See Adina Schwartz, pp. 634–46.

[6]See Robert Nozick, *Anarchy, State and Utopia* (New York: Basic Books, 1974), pp. 248–50.

self-development of employees in the workplace and the necessity that those in the position to do so assist in this self-development. Participation is a specific extension of that right, appropriately claimed by employees who are willing and capable of such involvement. Meaningful work, including participatory management, fulfills the promise not merely of employment but of purposeful employment and thus contributes to employee self-development. This right does not conflict with or supersede freedom of contract. Rather, it is parallel to this freedom, and balances the privileges of freedom of contract. Such rights balance employer freedoms because in general, managers, particularly those in a position to hire and fire, enjoy more freedom to develop and to control their own jobs than do other employees. Participatory management and meaningful work programs provide equal opportunities for the exercise of these sorts of freedoms for *all* employees.

Why is such balancing, and thus the positive right to freedom, necessary or even desirable in the workplace? Freedom of choice and self-control over one's own life remain merely theoretical until an opportunity is provided for their active exercise. But such opportunities, so important to rational adults, are often absent in the workplace. Meaningful work and participation in business decisions contribute to one's sense of dignity and self-worth—to one's self-identity as a person. A job one considers menial, boring, or unduly degrading is damaging to self-respect. A job in which one has no control, where one has no contributory input, or that one perceives as menial is not merely demeaning, but is moreover detrimental to a sense of autonomy, self-independence, and free choice. Working is necessary for most of us and we place much importance on jobs in our evaluation of our own worth and that of others. In a society where mere survival is not an issue, it should be possible to make work meaningful for most employees and to develop participatory management.

Participation in the Workplace: An Example

To see what is entailed in meaningful work and participatory management, let us examine one participation project that tries to combine the ideals of meaningful work and participatory management with the goals of a profitable organization. In the 1970s the Harmon Auto Mirror Factory in Bolivar, Tennessee restructured its whole factory on a model of worker self-management. The project, called the Bolivar Project, involved management, union participation, and outside consultants from labor, business, and academia. The experiment was unusual because it involved reorganizing an entire factory rather than just one department or division. It depended on the active participation of union experts to reorganize the existing unionized work force. And it involved revamping an existing organizational structure that had been in place for many years, rather than designing a plant and carefully selecting manpower prepared for such an experiment. The goals of the project were to enhance the quality of the working environment and to increase productivity. The most important goal of the project was to turn the Bolivar plant into a model of industrial democracy where workers and management would participate on all levels of decision-making.

To this end four principles governing the project were advocated: (1) security of job and safety, (2) equity of job development, compensation, and work rules for everyone at the plant, (3) democracy in the decision-making processes, and (4) individuation—the idea that every person is different and therefore should be treated differently in the workplace. Goals (3) and (4) were the most innovative in the project. Democratization involved the formation of worker-management committees that decided work standards and pay scales, and developed job descriptions and incentive programs. In addition every person in each department was invited to evaluate the work procedure, to experiment with new work techniques, to exchange jobs, and to criticize each other and the committee. Employees could use extra time to participate in plant job training programs designed to enhance employee development. The management, too, had to be trained not to be merely managers but facilitators to see to it that every employee who wished to do so could contribute to management decision-making.

The task of individuation was most difficult. It was impossible to respond to the needs and goals of every person in the plant individually. But studies showed that there were six main personality types in the plant, each characterized by certain common work attitudes, needs, and job goals. By focusing on these six types the Bolivar project teams were able to adjust working conditions and incentives to meet many of the needs of the workers. For example, one group was union-oriented. These were encouraged to participate in the union's role in the project. Another group were hard-working craftspersons. To these was given the difficult work that satisfied their desires. Another group of craftsmen were more relaxed, enjoying their co-workers as much as their work. This group liked the freedom to choose work hours, organize their division, and in general were the group most critical of hierarchical management and most receptive to participatory programs. A fourth group were labeled the "sociables." Their work satisfaction came largely from identification and even dependence on social relationships with other employees. This group needed a strong sense of belonging, thrived on approval of their work, and did not want to take leadership roles. The most difficult group were the "farmer-workers," persons who had had to take jobs because they could no longer be self-supporting. They were the most troublesome from the perspective of the goals of the project because they did not enjoy working and were receptive neither to unionization nor to participation programs. The most interesting but not the easiest group were the "ambitious." These persons were the most motivated to be leaders but were not interested in participatory management. Their views were typified by the maxim that those who are smart, efficient, and hard-working will succeed; thus those in management deserve to be there. The challenge was to channel this ambition into satisfactory work outlets that would not conflict with the effort to restructure the hierarchy of management.

What is most reassuring about this project is that the Harmon Auto Mirror Factory is still operating, and operating profitably. The participatory program is still in place. Some hierarchical management positions have been reinstated, and not all workers at Harmon are completely satisfied. But the prevailing judgment is that the program has achieved its aims to increase productivity, worker satisfaction, and participation without sacrificing success in the market.[7]

The Harmon plant is a single example, and one must be careful not to overgeneralize. But Harmon does show that participatory management in a unionized plant with a diverse work force and a variety of jobs can be both possible and practical. Hopefully other businesses will try this sort of project in the future.

OBJECTIONS AND DEFENSES OF PARTICIPATION
IN THE WORKPLACE

A number of objections have been raised to participation projects. One should emphasize that almost no one objects to the *principle* that every person should be allowed to develop freely and that every person should have a meaningful job. Rather, the objections are based on the following contentions.

1. Participation is not a right but rather a privilege earned by the most capable.
2. The institution of such programs interferes with the rights of employers and employees freely to associate and operate.
3. Supervisors and managers will lose their jobs as a result of employee participation.
4. Worker participation programs lead to a loss of productivity and/or profits because workers lack the technical skills and management training necessary to participate wisely in corporate decision-making and may make short-term self-interested decisions that will harm the profitability and long-term viability of the company.
5. Some types of participation programs give unions further powers to intrude

---

[7]Michael Maccoby, "Changing Work: The Bolivar Project," *Working Papers*, Summer 1975, pp. 43–54, and Agis Salpukas, "Bolivar: A Reporter's View," *The New York Times*, April 9, 1975, rpt. in Maccoby, pp. 46–47.

into the management of corporations,[8] leading to radical egalitarianism and worker control.

6. Finally, like other objections to employee rights, critics are afraid that participatory management will be the end of freedom of contract and thus voluntarism in the market place.

The first objection questions participation as a positive right. It suggests that if everyone is left alone to compete in the workplace without interference, those who are most capable will naturally assume positions of management. But there are a number of problems with this position. Without the right to participate in the workplace some workers will never be allowed the opportunity or "privilege" for self-development. If our society were truly perfect so that every person had equal opportunities, equal education, and equal chances to attain management positions, the claim that participation is merely an earned privilege would have some merit. But this is not the case. Education and opportunities are not equally distributed, and much success is a matter of chance or social opportunity. Positive programs to enhance self-development are essential to equalize opportunities and to allow each person the option to participate in the workplace. Objection 2 recalls defenses of EAW, to which we responded in Chapter Four.

In response to the third and fourth objections, I would point out that worker participation is not necessarily the same thing as worker *control* and the demise of management. Supervisors and managers will not lose their jobs if workers are allowed to participate in management decision-making. They will merely lose their alleged right to control everything that happens in the workplace. Well-informed participation on many levels has often enhanced the economic well-being of corporations that have tried such programs. Moreover, the institution of meaningful work programs does not mean that no one will do menial or repetitive tasks. Rather, innovative programs seek ways to reduce or to fairly share such tasks while maintaining or increasing productivity. From this utilitarian perspective, a recent book, *In Search of Excellence,* suggests that one of the characteristics of a profitable, stable company is that it involves every employee in the business of the corporation. When employees identify with their jobs and participation is encouraged at all levels of decision-making, the author argues, the result is a level of excellence that can be measured in both economic and moral terms.[9] Consequently, participatory management, which involves worker decision-making and input on all levels and thus has the effect of

[8]See, for example, Herbert Northrup, "Worker Participation, Industrial Democracy or Union Power Enhancement?" a public speech, reprinted in Alan F. Westin and Stephan Salisbury, eds., *Individual Rights in the Corporation* (New York: Pantheon Books, 1980), pp. 358–64.

[9]See *In Search of Excellence,* especially Chapter One.

"flattening the management hierarchy," is not contrary to the profit orientation of free enterprise.

Fifth, participation programs in the workplace are often wrongly identified with the Yugoslavian model of self-management in which every worker participates fully in the management of the company whether or not he wants to or has the capacity to. The result of this egalitarian organization of the work force is that untrained and inexperienced persons have become managers, Yugoslav productivity is low, and profits are unknown. This result is undesirable even from the perspective of the Yugoslavian worker because many businesses do not produce enough to support their workers, and the quality of products is often mediocre.

But participation programs need not, and indeed should not, be modeled on the Yugoslavian plan. Not everyone is either capable or desirous of management decision-making, and no participatory management program will be successful unless participants are well-trained in management skills. Participatory management programs must take into account the abilities and desires of different employees. Those interested in management should be given training opportunities. Those who are unfit for or do not want to participate in the management process should be left alone. This does not mean that they should be left to do what they perceive as menial tasks, but instead that they should be helped to find work that is meaningful to them.

Finally, participation programs in this country should be cooperative management-worker ventures, not enforced egalitarian reconstructions of the workplace. To sacrifice employer freedoms for the sake of worker satisfaction is as unfair to business as the sacrifice of employee rights for employer prerogatives is unfair to employees. As we have repeatedly argued in this book, instituting employee rights in the workplace is an extension, rather than an abrogation, of the voluntarism so valued in our society. Freedom of contract is not threatened by participatory management. Rather, the kinds of voluntary choices employees must make in order to work are enhanced by an improvement in the quality of work life and the opportunity for true autonomy as a valued and valuable person rather than merely a laborer. In a voluntary cooperative program of employee development respect for employee rights, worker satisfaction, profit, and productivity can all be achieved without sacrificing any one for the sake of the others.

APPENDIX

Specific Programs

A PROGRAM FOR WORKER SAFETY

An employee-employer program for worker safety might include the following stipulations.

1. Employees have a right to information about work hazards. This requires the following provisions.
   a. Employers should be held liable for being well-informed about hazards and dangers in their industry.
   b. Employees should be fully informed about possible as well as real work dangers before taking a job or being transferred to a job. If dangers are inherent in the job, the long-term risks should be spelled out in detail in advance of hiring.
   c. Employees should be informed of their legal rights to protest or to object to work dangers.
2. Because employees have a right to safety, and because employers have the right to be protected from employee negligence and abuse of safety regulations, the following rules should be instituted.
   d. Employees should participate in improving worker safety. This should include on-site studies of worker safety and working conditions conducted periodically by worker-management teams or committees.
   e. Conscientious objection: workers should be allowed to protest or refuse what they think is unsafe work without penalty. However, their protest should be examined by an employee-management committee, and the supposed danger should be documented by an outside expert.
   f. No worker should be penalized for conscientious objection unless he or she refuses to return to work when the danger is alleviated or proven unfounded. Any worker found habitually using conscientious objection as an excuse not to work should be dismissed.

    g. The worker-management committee should also adjudicate work-er negligence. Careless workers or workers who refuse to take prescribed safety precautions should be transferred or dismissed.

3. Legal Remedies:

    h. Preventable work hazards should be prohibited by law.

    i. Employee rights to refuse unsafe work should be protected by statute.

    j. Employers should be encouraged to improve working conditions with tax incentives or workers' compensation payment reductions that reward safe places of work.

A PROGRAM FOR EMPLOYEE INFORMATION
AND COMMUNICATION IN THE WORKPLACE

1. Employees should have full access to personnel information about themselves.

2. Employees should be fully informed about employee benefits and lia-bilities such as health plans, pension benefits, stock options, and employee rights.

3. Employees have the right to full information about their job and the future of their position in the company.

4. Employees have the right to as much information as is possible about their company, e.g., financial data, inventory, sales, profits, etc., without divulging company secrets. Employees should not be denied information available to nonemployees such as stockholders or investors.

5. Employees misusing company information should be dismissed.

6. A policy of free-flowing information and communication on all corpo-rate levels enhances job development, increases employee loyalty, and often prevents costly errors.

PROGRAMS FOR PARTICIPATION IN THE WORKPLACE

Worker participation, although not wide-spread, takes many forms in our country. These include the following.

1. Worker, employee, or union representation on boards of directors. (Chrysler has such representation.)

2. Corporate reform through stockholder proposals where worker-share-holders vote in blocks. To date this sort of participation has not been successful because workers do not have majority interests in companies.

3. Union bargaining for employee rights and employee participation.

4. Profit sharing. (See the Scanlon Plan described in the next section.)

5. Participatory Management. Worker committees or worker-manage-ment committees share and manage segments of the corporation. (See the Bolivar Project.)

6. Worker-management safety committees. These committees encourage worker participation and cooperative interest in learning about work

hazards and in improving the safety of the workplace, and discourage worker negligence as well.

7. Worker-owned companies. There a few of these, e.g., The Chicago-Northwestern Railroad. However these experiments have not been altogether successful, partly because companies willing to sell to their employees are by and large in such poor financial condition that it is difficult for inexperienced workers to improve their financial viability.

The Scanlon Plan

One of the most widely accepted and successful worker participation programs is a proposal called the Scanlon Plan. Scanlon was an open-hearth steel worker in the 1930s. While at work he noticed falling productivity and inefficiencies in the plant where he was working and he convinced his employer to adopt a plan whereby labor and management would work as a team to improve working conditions and employee productivity and at the same time try to settle employee grievances. The plan, thereafter called the Scanlon Plan, has three parts.

1. Programs of participation, cooperation and frankness will be instituted on all levels of employment between workers and supervisors.
2. Committees will be formed that include employees and supervisors from each area, section, or plant division. These committees will make suggestions on ways to improve productivity, the quality of work, efficiency, and other job-related phenomena.
3. When performance improves in a given section of the company bonuses, paid monthly to increase incentives, are awarded to that section.

The aim of the Scanlon Plan is participation, a share in the profits of the corporation as an incentive for improved work, and the development of identity with one's job. The plan does not solve all problems of participation, but where it has been tried it has been highly successful in achieving the aims of the company and creating more satisfactory working relationships.[1]

[1]Harold E. Lane, "The Scanlon Plan Revisited," *Business and Society Review,* 16 (1975–76), pp. 57–64.

8

Implied Contracts in Employment: The Prima Facie Right Not to Be Fired

The right to due process insures that if due process procedures are fair and objective employees will not be dismissed or demoted without appeal. Employee rights to freedom and privacy assert that workers cannot be fired for legitimately exercising or demanding these entitlements. The right to safety assures minimal decent conditions for working. The absence of any one of these in the workplace is inconsistent with society's claim to extend equal rights to all citizens. Further, the rights to meaningful work and participation expand employee rights to include positive freedoms for worker self-development. In this final chapter I shall further expand employee rights, arguing that there are implied contracts in employment, specifically the prima facie moral right of permanent employees not to be fired without good reason. This right is of different status than the other employee rights we have defended. It is not a basic right without which there would be no employee entitlements but, rather, a substantive right to due process that entails not merely the procedural guarantee of employer explanation and employee appeal for questionable employment practices, but also requires that such explanations and appeals provide *good* reasons. This right alleviates some injustices in the workplace that favor the employer at the expense of the employee, and it does so without disturbing traditional property arrangements. Most importantly, the recognition of this right answers the critics of capitalism who contend that private ownership creates and cannot eradicate injustices in the workplace. Thus while other employee rights grant workers moral rights that every person should have, the right not to be fired extends the principles of fairness and justice in the workplace.

Before defending implied contracts in employment, one crucial fact must be emphasized. In the climate of the 1980s, where the ownership and management of corporations is divided, some mature corporations recognize the value of the loyalty and experience of "at will" employees, or at least of middle managers and executives. Arbitrary dismissal is *not* a common occurrence; in fact it more often happens that corporations keep loyal long-term managers even when their contributions to the corporation are diminishing. The reason for this attitude is not only that some legislation prohibits dismissal because of age. Most if not all persons at all levels in corporations are themselves employees, so senior managers are at least sympathetic with the positions of their peers. Thus many major corporations recognize their moral obligations to some long-term employees, obligations that go beyond their "at will" legal duties. What is to be argued in the following sections is that implied contracts should be recognized as such and should be extended to all long-term productive loyal employees.

IMPLIED CONTRACTS IN EMPLOYMENT

> L. J. Hablas was an employee for almost forty-three years at Armour and Company. At various times during his career Hablas had considered quitting Armour, but he had been dissuaded by his supervisors for a number of reasons, including the promise of a nice pension at retirement. However, at age fifty-nine, six months before he was eligible to retire with pension, Hablas was dismissed. Because Hablas was an "at will" employee he was not eligible to receive any retirement pay from Armour. Although the courts found that there was no justifiable reason for Hablas' dismissal, they nevertheless upheld the right of Armour to dismiss Hablas on the basis that Hablas had been repeatedly reminded of his "at will" status, which allowed him to quit whenever he wished, just as it also allowed Armour to dismiss him.[1]

Although Armour had the legal right to fire him under the principle of EAW, one nevertheless must sympathize with Hablas who had worked for the company for forty-three years without being fired. Sympathy for Hablas is, however, not enough to make a strong *philosophical* case for his defense. Are there any moral rights to one's job, rights one has because one has been a decent and loyal employee for a number of years? To establish that there are, a number of arguments will have to be mustered.

Hablas' treatment may be questioned on a number of grounds. First, if one accepts our previous thesis that EAW is an unjust principle, Hablas' firing was unfair, because he was dismissed without due process. Now this

[1]*Hablas* v. *Armour and Company*, 270 F. 2d 71 (1959).

book has contended that EAW *is* an unjust principle, that the arguments criticizing EAW are valid, and that EAW should be abolished as a common-law principle. But putting these arguments aside, something more is at stake here. For the issue is not merely Hablas' effectiveness as an employee, a question that would have been resolved in a grievance procedure, but rather his value as a loyal employee, a loyalty that evolved in forty-three years with the company. Moreover, I shall argue that, even setting aside the injustices of EAW, one can make a plausible argument for an implied contract in employment on the basis of the reciprocal nature of accountability in the workplace.

Earlier we argued that employer-employee relationships are not merely economic in nature. Employees are persons. When one hires workers one hires persons, not merely productive robots. Simply by hiring a person an employer enters into a moral relationship. Because moral accountability relationships are reciprocal in character, a point elaborated in Chapter Five, an employer, having entered into an employment relationship with an employee, is responsible, morally responsible, to the employee, just as the employee is accountable to the employer. On the crudest and most basic level, employees are expected to come to work on time, to do an adequate job, to work the required hours, and not to steal from the company. Thus employees are held accountable for minimal moral decency at work just as they are held accountable for being economically productive. These obligations are implied when employees are hired. In return, the employer is expected to treat the employee with at least minimal decency and respect. Notice that the ways in which an employer is accountable to an employee are not identical to the correlative employee-to-employer relationship. But employers cannot avoid being morally accountable to their employees.

What is the nature of this correlative accountability? Obviously it includes treating employees with respect and dignity as rational adults, just as employees are expected to treat employers. It includes upholding employee political rights to due process, freedom, and privacy in the workplace; and it includes periodic job reviews, providing information to employees about their long-term status in the company, and instituting plans for making work meaningful. These points have been argued in earlier chapters. This is where the notion of an implied contract enters the relationship. If a long-time relationship develops between an employer and a permanent employee, and if the employee receives adequate job reviews and is not dismissed, a moral contract or bond arises between the two. The employer continues to anticipate adequate and even improved employee performance, and, in return, despite their "at will" *legal* relationship, the employee expects, at the least, job security. Such employee expectations are not unwarranted. A long-time employee has been expected to be loyal and productive, she has supported the company, she has adjusted to company changes, and she has not quit. If her expectations of job security are supported by positive reviews, raises, and promotions there is an implication, although admittedly not a requirement, that this employment is permanent. This is clearly a moral, not a legal, expectation. (There are legal contracts of this sort, but I am now talking about unwritten contracts between "at will" employees and employers.) Long-term "at will" employment, then, implies a moral expectation: the reciprocity of respect and job security in return for continued loyalty and productivity. This is an implied moral contract.

When an employer such as Armour fires a long-term employee such as Hablas, it breaks an implied agreement. The agreement is not broken only with the employee in question, for Hablas is a symbol for the relationship that exists or should exist between the employer and all of its employees. Armour must have sensed this, and that is probably why the company fought the case. They did not want to be held responsible, even under an implied nonenforceable agreement, for long-term employees. They wanted to demonstrate that under EAW such a moral agreement did not exist between themselves and their employees.

Why would an employer want to recognize such implied contracts in employment? For the very reasons we have mentioned earlier—to honor employees as rational adults, or, on a more practical level, to reinforce expected employee decency, loyalty and efficiency. When an employer such as Armour fails to honor a contract with one person it is, in effect, declaring the so-called contract null and void for all its "at will" employees. Surely such declarations harm employee morale. If implied contracts are not recognized, the moral basis of the relationship between employees and employers weakens. Employers then threaten the logic of their demands on employee moral decency, for why should an employee be expected to act in a morally sensitive manner at work when she is not treated with respect by her employer? Moreover, when the moral employee-employer contract of loyalty breaks down, relationships take on an adversary character, a character not atypical of many employee-management relationships existing today. Such situations invite coercive regulation or legislation.

The arguments defending implied contracts in employment do not prove beyond a reasonable doubt that employees have a prima facie right not to be fired, or even that employees who have been with a company for a long time have such a right. They argue, rather, for the moral reasonableness of such a contract for long-term productive employees. Reciprocal moral relationships between employees and employers require job security, and thus that employers have duties, *moral* duties, to honor implied contracts to such job security. Without this, moral accountability in the workplace falls apart.

Proponents of this thesis will contend that the principle of an implied contract in employment should be extended to "protected" workers as well, in particular, those covered by collective bargaining agreements. This is so, but those persons have built-in bargaining arrangements or protections with which they can negotiate such issues. "At will" employees do not. If one can make a sound case for unprotected employees, the same justifications should be equally useful in defending implied contracts for protected employees.

ARGUMENTS FROM THE RIGHT TO OWNERSHIP

Some philosophers will be dissatisfied with the foregoing discussion. They will want *proof* that employees have positive rights not to be fired. Such proofs are difficult, but a more stringent argument might use the right to private ownership as a basis for justifying substantive rights in employment.

Let us examine carefully the right to ownership. In the Introduction we said that the right to private ownership is a conventional but very important right in any capitalist economy. There we said that ownership entails at least a three-term relation between the claimant (the owner or prospective owner), the object claimed (property), and others who are in a position to make a similar claim, that is, persons who might want that property as well.[2] Let us explore the right to ownership further. At least sometimes, ownership entails a fourth relationship, the relationship between owners and nonclaimants who are affected by the power and position of the ownership claim. For instance, ownership gives a corporation certain powers, which include the power to offer employment. This fourth sort of relationship arises when an owner or a manager is in a position to extend employment and remuneration to others who, in turn, will be expected to enhance the business. Ownership, then, may place persons or institutions such as corporations in a position to affect the rights of others to work and to be paid. Ownership may also increase the value of what is owned, without any further acquisition taking place, because of the productivity of employees who contribute to the business. Therefore employee-employer relationships are reciprocal relationships on the economic level of exchange as well on the moral level, because while an owner is able to offer employment and thus a means of survival to certain persons, the exchange is hardly one-sided. On the other side an employee creates an analogous but different relationship with the employer by accepting a job,

[2]Joyotpaul Chaudhuri, "Toward a Democratic Theory of Property and the Modern Corporation," *Ethics*, 81 (1971), pp. 271–86.

since the presence of an employee and his or her work changes and usually improves the business of the employer. This is a reciprocal trade. The employer *needs* the employee to develop production, just as the employee needs the employer in order to have a job.

One of the strongest objections to a capitalist economic system is the contention that the right to private ownership, which forms the basis of that sort of economy, creates inequalities that are to the advantage of the owner and to the disadvantage of the nonowner. But disadvantages are not created merely because of the abstract right to ownership. Private owner- ship is, in theory at least, an equal right so that in principle everyone has a *right* to own property and has that right equally. Nor do disadvantages necessarily arise just because of an unequal *distribution* of what is owned. The difficulty, rather, is that property places some persons in positions of authority over the rights of nonowners to jobs and to fair pay, and this authority can be abused to the unfair disadvantage of employees who are not in a position to control or stop this abuse.

The traditional free enterprise owner-employee relationship has radi- cally changed. In this country in the twentieth century almost every worker is the employee of a corporation. The owners of corporations are absent shareholders who exert little or no authority over the business, while the actual running of the corporation is done by hired managers who need not own shares in the company. Many of the rights previously exercised by owners have been transferred to executives, managers, and others in the position to hire and fire other employees. In the absence of a single owner, managers are put in positions of power over those under them, whom they can hire and fire at will and treat in other ways as they please, even though they themselves must report to other executives, who can exercise similar powers over them. Therefore in the modern corporation many employees are accorded the role of "employer" in employment relations, just as if they were in fact the real owners of the corporation. This whole arrangement, in a complex way, continues an ownership-power arrangement.

What is wrong with this arrangement? Despite the fact that employers need employees, employers, that is, owners or managers, are placed in a different position than employees in regard to rights. As owners or manag- ers of an enterprise that provides means for work, employers are in a position of greater power than employees. This is not, by itself, necessarily *unfair* to the employee, but in fact unfairness does often enter the rela- tionship. Because of their positions, managers control the employment and job development of employees. By implied threats alone they can coerce employees into action not of their choosing. Of course employees can quit. But quitting and finding other employment is often difficult, at best. Im- plied threats to job security give employers undeniable leverage over em- ployees. This leverage may be to the unfair disadvantage of unprotected employees, because as we argued in Chapter Four, these employees have no counteracting leverage or redress in response to their employer-superior. This is not to imply that managers regularly exercise this power, or exercise it unwisely, but its availability is a constant temptation to managers, and a constant threat to "at will" employees.

In the Introduction we suggested that all rights are equal rights. Inequalities in a society are just only if they do not countenance the unequal exercise of rights to the disadvantage of some persons in that society. In a free enterprise economy, ownership rights are, in theory, equal rights, but in being exercised they may countenance unequal powers disadvantageous to employees, as we discussed earlier in Chapter Four. One could balance the inequality of power by abolishing private property, but a less radical way would be to grant employees who are loyal and productive a different but equal right: the prima facie right not to be fired.

What sort of right would this be, and how would it balance unfair inequalities created by private enterprise? The right might be stated as a substantive right to due process.

> After an apprenticeship of eight to ten years, an "at will" employee has a prima facie right to his or her job. This is an implied contract that cannot be broken except for "good reason." "Good reason" or due cause for firing, transfer, or demotion includes inability to perform the job for which one was hired, misbehavior connected with or on the job, such as tardiness, drunkenness, disrespect of fellow employees, lying about or to one's employer, stealing, and other obviously unacceptable behavior.[3]
>
> Due cause might include other moral factors such as discriminating against fellow employees or job applicants, failure to report quality problems to supervisors, carrying out environmentally harmful or wasteful activities in disregard to public policy, bribing officials in foreign countries, and other sorts of questionable activities. Further an employer has the right to dismiss an employee for documented economic reasons such as the transfer of the company when the employee is unwilling to move. An employer has the right to dismiss employees for severe financial reasons such as bankruptcy, so long as these economic reasons are publicly accountable.

The prima facie right not to be fired gives employees substantive claims not to be demoted or fired without good reasons. It promotes rationality in employer decisions, a highly valued quality of free enterprise, because it demands justification for employer judgments and thus logic in employee treatment. It balances possible disadvantages created by the exercise of unequal ownership-power arrangements in employment, because it expands nonowners' rights in the workplace by giving them a limited right to their jobs. Moreover, this right is not as outrageous a claim as one might think on first reading. A right to one's job is a logical although not an absolute entitlement. The following example illustrates why this is so.

[3]See J. Peter Shapiro and James F. Tune, "Implied Contract Rights to Job Security," *Stanford Law Review*, 26, Pt. 1 (1973–4), pp. 335–69.

If I rent an apartment and paint it, I certainly do not have a right to the apartment or to the walls I have improved, but if I do the work I do have a right to the improvement of the room created by the painting. This is because the apartment decoration is a direct result of my contribution of labor, without which the apartment would be as drab as when I first moved in. When I leave the apartment I even have a right to flake off the paint and restore the room to its original condition. By analogy, when I work I do not have the right to the employer's business. That is hers. I do not have a right to whatever I improve with my labor, because the raw materials upon which I work are not mine. Further, I am paid for my productivity, so I trade that and its products for remuneration. But, I am suggesting, I do have a right to the enhancing, to the working itself. It seems to me that working is just that—a productive or enhancing activity. It is not a thing, like an apartment or a product. When I am offered a job, I am offered an opportunity to contribute to someone else's business. The enhancement, the contribution to the business, belongs to the employer, and I am paid for part of that contribution, but the productive activity belongs to me. To argue that one has a prima facie right not to be fired is to recognize an employee's claim to his productive activity when that activity contributes positively and for a long period of time to the business of the employer.

Does this argument imply that employees have *property* rights to their jobs, as some of the recent literature on employee rights suggests?[4] I think this is the wrong analogy. Persons have rights to their jobs because the activity of working, an activity necessary for productivity, belongs to the person. Working is intrinsically part of, and cannot be separated from, a person in the way in which property can. Rights to jobs are not property rights because, as we argued in detail in criticizing the doctrine of EAW, persons are not property, nor do we want to think of them as such since this opens up the opportunity to defend voluntary slavery. Because persons are *not* forms of property, violations of the rights of persons are more serious, much more serious, than violations of property rights. Consequently, denying rights in employment is a much more serious matter than taking away someone's property since the latter is not part of a person while the former is. In not recognizing that long-term productive employees have rights to their jobs one is rejecting the contribution of that productive activity, an activity that has been identified with the employee's job and has for so long contributed to the production of the employer. A prima facie right not to be fired recognizes that which properly belongs to employees—their working.

---

[4]See for example, Philip J. Levine, "Towards a Property Right in Employment," *Buffalo Law Review*, 22 (1973), pp. 1081–1110. Donald H. J. Hermann, "Property Rights in One's Job: The Case for Limiting Employment-At-Will," *Arizona Law Review*, 24 (1983), pp. 901–57. David Ewing, *Do It My Way or You're Fired* (New York: John Wiley & Sons, Inc., 1982), pp. 241–87.

OBJECTIONS TO RIGHTS IN EMPLOYMENT

An objection to the notion of a prima facie right not to be fired is that, even more than other employee rights, this alleged right creates an imbalance of freedoms. The employee or the lower-ranking worker has the right to quit whenever he or she pleases, but the employer or higher-ranking employee losses the absolute right to fire whomever and whenever he or she pleases.[5] I would argue, however, that these freedoms of the employer or senior manager to fire when they please lead to an inequality of relationships, because the person in the position to fire has power over the fired person and may exercise this power "at will" over the employee. An employee is never in such a position. Therefore employer prerogatives are balanced by the employee's prima facie right not to be fired.

A second objection purports that if employees are given rights to their jobs, efficiency and productivity will suffer. There will be no incentive for employees to give their best efforts in the workplace if they cannot be fired. The work force will include lazy and unproductive persons, and those interested in working will have little incentive to do so. If it were the case that a right not to be fired was an absolute right, this objection would be correct. What has been argued is rather that loyal, efficient and productive employees have prima facie rights to the job for which they are hired. The employer has the right, and indeed the obligation, to fire or demote undeserving employees where "undeserving" is defined to include laziness and nonproductivity, so long as the employer follows due process procedures and can verify its accusations. What is required is that employers hire and evaluate carefully their apprentices so that their commitments to employees are as loyal and serious as the employee's commitment to the business.

GUARANTEEING RIGHTS IN EMPLOYMENT

How does one guarantee rights in employment? In many European countries they are guaranteed by law and enforced by the government. In Germany, for example, after a trial period employees have rights to their jobs. Persons may be dismissed for job-related negligence, absences, disruptive order, and criminal activities. The grounds for dismissal must be documented and hearings are conducted before an employee is fired. The United States is, in fact, the only major industrial nation that offers little protection of employees' rights to their jobs. It has been suggested that

[5]Donald L. Martin, "Is an Employee Bill of Rights Needed?" in Alan F. Westin and Stephen Salisbury, eds., *Individual Rights in the Corporation* (New York: Random House, 1980), pp. 15–20.

what is needed in this country is the kind of statutory protection for employees against unjust firing that is embodied in the German law.[6] It has been further suggested that this statutory protection should include rights to expenses incurred in finding a new job, and rights to back pay for those unjustly dismissed.[7]

A second way to guarantee employee rights is through written contracts between employers and employees, which state the exchange agreement, the rights of each party, and the means for enforcing these rights, such as arbitration, peer review, outside negotiators, etc. Explicit agreements would enforce the moral rights of each party and settle many disagreements about employee *and* employer rights out of court.

A third and less coercive way to institutionalize recognition of employee rights is simply for employers to do so voluntarily. Despite objections to this suggestion, one needs to consider it carefully. Increasingly, employees are demanding rights in the workplace; employers are beginning to recognize the expedience and, sometimes, the fairness of such demands; and the courts are beginning to take a positive interest in employee rights. There is an obvious way for employers to avoid "coercive intervention" by government and by the courts. This is for employers to institute programs that respect and protect employee rights on their own initiative.

CONCLUSION

The prima facie right not to be fired is not a basic moral right of the same status as other basic moral rights. Rather, it is a proposal for substantive due process that requires good reasons for decisions in employment practices. Substantive due process adjusts inequalities created by private free enterprise that are to the advantage of employers and to the unfair disadvantage of employees, so that every person receives fair treatment and equal consideration in the workplace. By means of an arrangement such as an implied contract in employment, capitalism would meet some of the criteria for a just as well as an efficient economic system.

[6]See Clyde B. Summers, "Individual Protection Against Unjust Dismissal: Time for a Statute," *Virginia Law Review*, 62, (1976), pp. 481–532.

[7]Lawrence E. Blades, "Employment at Will v. Individual Freedom: On Limiting the Abusive Exercise of Employer Power," *Columbia Law Review*, 67 (1967), pp. 1404–35.

Conclusion: Institutionalizing Moral Agency in Corporations

This book will conclude with a consideration of two sorts of questions. First, it has been argued that corporations have rights and responsibilities and can, as secondary moral agents, be held accountable. But traditionally corporations have not always acted as secondary moral agents. How might corporations operate so that moral awareness becomes an active, normal, even habitual part of corporate activity and thus of corporate character? Second, rights of corporations are derived from, and thus are related to and dependent upon, individual rights. On the other hand, employment, in the context of which employee rights, or their absence, becomes an issue depends on those who control the means of production. This control is by and large in the hands of corporations. Consequently, although the rights of corporations are by and large secondary claims, primary individual rights in the workplace develop in employment relationships made possible by corporations. Therefore, the rights as well as role responsibilities of both employees and corporations depend upon one another. If this is the case in an abstract way, how can mutual relationships be practically instituted in the modern corporation so that the rights of *each* party are respected? Can such mutual respect develop voluntarily within free enterprise? These questions are not unrelated to the first one, because the institution of corporate moral activity depends on the moral activity of constituents. Strong corporate-constituent correlative moral relationships should allow the realization of equal employee and employer rights and thus corporate moral awareness should develop.

DEVELOPMENT OF CORPORATE MORAL ACTIVITY

The contemporary literature on corporations offers a plethora of suggestions for the development of corporate moral activity, many of which are familiar to the reader.[1] In what follows I shall describe some of these proposals and then conclude with a model for corporate activities that outlines a framework in which employee rights can be recognized within corporations while preserving the freedom and autonomy of these institutions in a modern free enterprise economy. This plan calls for the voluntary development of corporate moral activity while at the same time respecting and enhancing the moral rights of both constituents *and* corporations.

ECONOMIC REFORMS

Let us begin by discussing briefly two "macro" alternatives that suggest remodeling the economy as a whole. These are:

1. Restore the economy to truly unregulated laissez-faire private free enterprise status.
2. Continue and increase regulation of corporations through legislation and regulatory agencies.

1. Unregulated Free Enterprise

A striking position on the issue of corporate responsibility and the future of business is that of economists such as Milton Friedman and others, who suggest that we return to an unregulated (laissez-faire) private free enterprise economy where each business regulates its internal affairs autonomously. According to this view, a private enterprise system unfettered by regulations preserves freedom and autonomy for corporations and thus for their constituents. Instead of expending time and money on regulation, such a system can invest its capital to promote economic growth. Lower taxes, possible because of reduced government, increase available capital. The rise of competition afforded by deregulation of prices, imports, and exports allows for growth, and with growth one sees an expanding job market, higher demand for workers, increased wages, and a better standard

---

[1]For a more complete list, see Thomas Donaldson, *Corporations and Morality* (Englewood Cliffs, N.J.: Prentice-Hall, Inc., 1981), Chapter 9.

of living for everyone. Moreover, according to this view, the power of unions and other employee activist groups and the trend towards enlightened corporate leadership in this century make it highly unlikely that the status of employees would return to the horrendous condition of the nineteenth century.[2] Finally, such an economy, according to some of its proponents, best preserves moral rights because it establishes the basic moral right to the negative freedom not to be coerced without encouraging positive rights that conflict with the freedom of others.

The problem with this scenario for the future of business is that it overlooks the most important, and often the most neglected aspect of modern business life: the relationship between the corporation and its human constituents. I would argue that *any* economic arrangement, including laissez-faire capitalism, would be workable if (a) it provides jobs, goods and services for a community, and (b) in doing so does not cause harm to the community. But (c) no economic arrangement is ethically satisfactory unless important moral rights are espoused and indeed flourish within that system in the following ways: (1) moral rights are embodied within the political structure in which the economy operates; and (2) these individual rights flourish within each component of that system, that is, within unions, businesses, and corporations, as well as within noneconomic institutions such as churches, schools, governmental agencies, and the like. This is because the institution of political rights in a society does not in itself guarantee that these rights will be recognized and honored everywhere throughout that society. This is illustrated by the fact that in this country political rights do not spill over into the workplace as we have seen. In light of the arguments proposed in support of EAW, it seems unlikely that a defender of that principle would seriously consider (c) as essential. But in order to be a just society, a society that truly honors moral rights, these must be espoused everywhere, and it is just this proliferation of rights that is ignored in the proposal for a return to a laissez-faire economy and by those who hold that all basic moral rights are merely negative rights.

2. Regulation and Legislation

A contrasting suggestion rejects the proposal of Friedman's camp on the grounds that it ignores employee rights and would not prevent possible negative side effects of unregulated business such as false advertising, the manufacture of defective products, pollution, misuse of natural resources, etc. According to this view, one needs to regulate business in these sensitive areas. This must be done by government, which can take an unbiased objective view of business in relation to the public interest. A version of this solution argues that we need legal statutes to create and protect employee

[2]Milton Friedman, *Capitalism and Freedom* (Chicago: University of Chicago Press, 1962, rpt. 1975).

rights and to protect society from corporate misbehavior. These statutes should protect one's right to a job and support other moral rights in the workplace such as those suggested in Part Two.[3]

This view, that regulation will solve societal problems, makes some rash assumptions. It supposes, wrongly, that because businesses have committed moral errors in the past, they are incapable of moral responsibility, and so must be regulated by laws and impartial government agencies. This supposition has been questioned in Part One. The question is *not* whether or not corporations are capable of moral responsibility. They are. The issue is how to recognize, encourage, and activate this moral activity. Secondly, this proposal assumes that governmental agencies always operate in a disinterested, fair, objective, and efficient manner. The history of these agencies belies this assumption. The inefficiencies of government regulation and its costs to government, to law enforcement agencies, to the courts, to taxpayers, and to business are shockingly great. Thirdly, regulation and legal sanctions will not enhance the *moral* activity of corporations, which simply respond to new regulations by obeying them to the letter of the law, as does Robotron. This proposal would improve corporate behavior on the surface, but it would be costly and would do little to encourage moral activities of business or to strengthen employee-employer relationships within the corporation.

CORPORATE REFORMS

Rather than change the economic system, a number of persons have suggested that a more fruitful approach to corporate moral development would be to institute reforms on a "micro" level, reforms involving changes of, or within, productive organizations. Such reforms range from legally mandated external restraints on corporations to voluntary restructuring mechanisms. We shall list some of these.

External Restraints
3. Limit the "life" of corporations by placing all corporations, or at least all large corporations, under federal charter.
4. Develop independent associations to regulate business.
5. Subject the corporation to an outside audit, or an outside social audit.
6. Subject the corporation to outside guardians who will control corporate behavior or even restructure the corporation.
7. Introduce enterprise liability and other market incentives to replace regulation where possible.

[3]See for example, Clyde B. Summers, "Individual Protection Against Unjust Dismissal: Time for a Statute," *Virginia Law Review,* 62, (1976), pp. 481–532.

With the exception of no. 7, these suggestions, like no. 2, merely impose more outside control on corporate activity without exploring the possibility that corporations might be able to act responsibly without such control. While federal charters and a restriction on the life of the corporation are feasible, there is no guarantee that they would change the nature of corporate behavior. And surely the last modicum of autonomy from political control would be gone when corporations were under the charter of the federal government or when the government was interfering with the market. If corporations have *any* claims to the rights of freedom and autonomy, these would be lost under these schemes.

Internal Reforms

8. Legislate (by law) the use of the business judgment rule, which allows corporations that act in good faith to exercise their own judgment in settling ethically questionable matters.

9. Institute an internal social audit or other evaluative measures within the corporation as part of standard corporate operating procedures. This could be voluntary or required by legislation.

10. Develop public methods for disclosure of corporate activities, holding corporate decision-makers legally liable for their actions.

All of these suggestions propose that corporate decisions should be made public and the decision-makers held legally liable for their actions. An example of such a policy is the recent Foreign Corrupt Practices Act, which requires corporations to make public illegal payments abroad, and mandates that persons involved in making bribes and paying extortion are to be held criminally liable for their actions.

These and other methods for holding corporate constituents publicly and legally liable for their actions are effective ways to force corporate interest in moral responsibility, because they are directed to the persons who are in charge of much of corporate decision-making. But social audits are hard to conduct, disclosure is sometimes hard to regulate, and legalizing such processes makes them hard to police without a great deal of governmental interference. On the other hand, private and voluntary programs of this sort might be successfully carried out if there were built-in accountability mechanisms in the corporations. I shall discuss this in the last sections of this chapter.

Reforms in the Membership and Duties
of Boards of Directors

11. Insist that the board of directors be made up of a majority of outsiders, e.g., union officials, church or academic leaders, or other disinterested persons.

12. Institute ethics committees and audit committees on the board of directors.

Solutions 11 and 12 are of interest, because they suggest what was argued more stringently earlier, that moral imput is a necessary condition for corporate moral responsiveness. Outside or disinterested directors would bring new moral considerations into the corporation, and an ethics committee would serve to emphasize this board role.[4] It is sometimes suggested that a lower-level employee and/or a union official be included on the board of directors so that worker rights as well as larger societal obligations come into the forefront of corporate considerations. Recently the Chrysler Corporation put a union official on its board of directors without negative results. Today most boards of directors of large corporations have a majority of outside directors, and many of them have active ethics committees. The difficulties with Solutions 11 and 12 are that (a) these changes in boards of directors often assure the observance of moral duties as spelled out by law, but do not guarantee moral behavior; and (b) somtimes these are the *only* steps taken to increase corporate moral activity. This is problematic because boards of directors tend to work only on large societal issues. They do not concentrate on the internal activities of a corporation and thus might not operate as a stimulant to increase employee rights and closer corporate-constituent relationships on the worker level.[5]

Specific Internal Ethical Programs

13. Install a Chief Executive Officer (CEO) of strong moral character whose overriding concern is moral excellence.
14. Institute positions within the corporation that represent the public, social, and/or employee interests, such as an ombudsperson, a vice president in charge of social responsibility, or a resident ethicist.
15. Institute training programs in ethical responsibility within the corporation.
16. Draw up codes of ethics for corporate employees.
17. Encourage the adoption of constitutions or bills of rights by each corporation.

The most idealistic and difficult means of instituting corporate moral awareness is through voluntary internal reforms within corporations. One of these might be strong "hands-on" moral leadership by top corporate executives, leadership without which the development of moral awareness is difficult to achieve.[6] Such leadership is important, but I would claim, not a sufficient condition for corporate moral change, because moral change must involve all levels of corporate decision-making to be truly effective. A strong CEO can be successful only if she can instill confidence, enthusiasm, and initiative throughout the organization. To find such a corporate leader

[4]See Ralph Nader and others, *The Taming of the Giant Corporation* (New York: W. W. Norton & Co., 1976).

[5]For other more negative criticisms of this idea, see Christopher Stone, *Where the Law Ends* (New York: Harper & Row Publishers, 1975), Chapters 14, 15, and 16.

[6]See Elmer Johnson, "Corporate Leadership and the Adversary Society" (unpublished essay); and Thomas J. Peters and Robert H. Waterman, Jr., *In Search of Excellence* (New York: Harper & Row, 1982).

is, at best, difficult and often a matter of luck. The appointment of personnel such as an ombudsperson or resident ethicists whose duties are to
represent public, social and/or employee interests is valuable, too, if these
persons are given sufficient power to effect corporate responsiveness to
ethical issues. Similarly, ethical training programs are useful if what is
taught is actually carried out in corporate action. The "if" is of course the
problem, and few corporate reformers have made concrete suggestions in
this area. In the next section I shall argue that internalizing moral decision-
making as part of corporate activities is more fruitful than training programs in ethics.

Often corporations draw up codes of ethics for employee behavior.
The problems with codes are two-fold. Codes usually tell the employee
what he or she is not permitted to do, but they seldom spell out worker
rights. Second, codes are often seen as laws. Employees, then, function
within the letter of the written code rather than take seriously their responsibilities in relation to the corporation and to society.

Solution 17 focuses specifically on the rights of employees in the
corporation, suggesting that corporations draw up constitutions in which
the rights of employees, management, stockholders, and the corporation
are all spelled out. Most proposals for constitutions suggest that the corporation adopt a bill of rights for employees. David Ewing, for example, in his
book *Freedom Inside the Organization,* proposes such a document.[7] The problem with many proposed bills of rights, as opposed to codes of ethics, is that
these bills spell out employee rights while neglecting employer claims. I
would suggest that if bills of rights are to be formulated, parallel rights for
employees *and* employers should be included. Such a document would
consist of a summary of employee rights, including those discussed in Part
Two, and would include a complete list of parallel employer rights as well.
The Appendix following the Conclusion is a sample of such a document.
Bills of rights are models for ideal employee-employer relationships, but
merely having a bill of rights does not guarantee that rights will be honored
in the workplace. Sometimes such bills are perceived as coercive "legalese"
by employers or even by employees, and sometimes are used as excuses not
to institute real reforms. Making bills of rights work is an issue not yet
resolved in the workplace.

18. A CORPORATE-CONSTITUENT MODEL FOR CORPORATE MORAL ACTIVITY

Strong CEOs, ethical awareness programs, protection of employee rights
through ombudspersons and resident ethicists, codes of ethics, and bills of
rights might contribute to developing a corporate moral character, but all of

---

[7]David Ewing, *Freedom Inside the Organization* (New York: McGraw-Hill Book Company,
1977), pp. 144–51.

these are "top down" mechanisms that must filter through the organization from top management. Thus they do not guarantee that every individual in the corporation will receive ethical 'benefits' from them, nor do they insure moral activity and the development of moral character throughout the corporation. Moreover, at least some of these suggestions entail a great deal of government regulation to be effective.

To conclude the essay I shall sketch another model for corporate moral agency, a model by which moral activities can be activated on all levels of business, and by which employee and employer rights can be realized freely and voluntarily without external coercion or government interference. This model will not be identical to a model of individual moral personhood because one cannot break down the corporate means-ends structure that is a peculiar and essential feature of these economic organizations without destroying them as profitable institutions. Moreover, as we argued in Part One, one does not want to personify the corporation so as to give it more in the way of moral personhood than human beings. The challenge will be to construct an ideal for corporate activity in which moral considerations are a natural part of decision-making and all constituents of the organization are treated as autonomous persons without destroying corporate economic functions and with them the reasons for corporate existence. The model I propose preserves the corporation as a viable profit-making organization while incorporating a framework for participatory management and voluntary structures for establishing meaningful work on all corporate levels. The existence of an independent board of directors, a strong, principled CEO, ombudspersons, codes of ethics, and bills of rights would support the framework I propose. But moral agency will operate in corporations continuously and habitually only if moral activities take place on all levels of corporate activity. My proposal takes into account this crucial dimension.

To activate moral activity in corporations while taking into account employee rights in the workplace there are certain minimal conditions. **1**. Changes must be made in the corporation-constituent relationship such that (**a**) each individual constituent makes a radical difference in a corporation, (**b**) each individual constituent is accountable for his or her business actions, and (**c**) the corporation is accountable to all of its constituents, including each of its employees. **2**. Changes must also be made in the relationship between corporate goals and constituent conduct. **3**. As a result of these changes, the choice and achievement of corporate goals must have a moral as well as an economic effect on constituents. Let us examine each of these points.

One will recall that in criticizing the definition of a corporation as a moral person it was noted that such a definition gave too much in the way of rights to corporations, so that a corporation might be able to exercise its freedom to a greater extent than, and sometimes to the disadvantage of, individuals. A second definition of a corporation as a formal organization defined an employee's role in an organization as an impersonal contributor to company productivity and profitability. One of the criticisms of that definition was that it ignored the fact that employees are persons who often contribute moral as well as economic input to corporate decision-making. In both of these definitions of the corporation, the individual constituent plays at best a secondary role in corporate activity. Further, one of the objections of EAW was that it sometimes led to the treatment of workers as if they were productive or nonproductive robots. Throughout this book, then, there has been sustained criticism of any organization, any law, or any principle that ignores or sacrifices the treatment of persons as rational adults. An essential reason for constituting corporations so that each individual constituent has a crucial role is to take into account that constituents are persons and deserve the dignity and respect rightly accorded persons. A second reason for emphasizing the role of individuals in corporate activities is the following. If our description of a corporation as a collective is correct, any corporate moral activity depends on the moral activity of its constituents. The moral (or immoral) input of each constituent contributes positively or negatively to moral or immoral decisions and thus to the "actions" of a corporation. Consequently it should matter whom one hires and retains, since that person's economic productivity *and* moral input contribute both to the profitability and to the character of the organization. If corporations want to remain or become more independent, this should be an important consideration.

Conditions (b) and (c) follow from our analysis of the reciprocal nature of employee-employer relationships. The point, in brief, is that one cannot hold employees accountable, morally accountable, without allowing them to call the corporation into account as well. Otherwise the obligatory force of the relationship breaks down. The specific ways in which a corporation may be held accountable to its constituents will be discussed in the paragraphs to follow.

Conditions 2 and 3 may appear to be strange sorts of conditions to demand of a free enterprise organization. However, they represent a further and more substantive extension of employee-employer relationships. If employees are to have recognized moral rights in the workplace, rights established voluntarily without legislation, employees must become integrated into the corporation is such a way that the organization is "their" organization. Its decisions are also employee decisions, and its goals should be employee goals as well. Otherwise there is a continued decay of employee-employer relationships, which could preclude a fully integrated and thus well-functioning organization. Further, if corporations are to be held morally accountable, then their constituents must be held accountable too, and must play an important role in choosing and changing the direction of the corporation. Keeping goals impersonally 'at a distance' from constituent input also places constituents 'at a distance' from the aims, directives, and activities of the corporation. Such a situation does not allow moral participation by constituents, and thus does not permit positive contributions to the moral development of corporate activities.

How might 1, 2, and 3 be achieved? Specifically, to establish corporate moral activity, the relationship between a corporation and its employees should be restructured so that each individual makes a significant difference to the organization in which she works. In such a model, employment in a corporation is similar to membership in a club or citizenship in a country. Hiring on all levels becomes a serious matter. A potential employee is expected to be morally as well as economically committed to the organization. That is, the constituent should find the "activities" of the corporation morally acceptable or at least amenable to changes that would make them morally acceptable to the constituent. A corporation, in turn, is expected to hire only those persons or groups of persons whom the corporation wishes to keep and develop over a long period of time.

Groups, teams, assembly lines, or divisions within the corporation should be organized so that the presence or absence of any one individual makes a marked difference to the "personality" and performance of the group. This is in part because of the ways in which employees are to be held individually accountable for their performance, but also because each team, group, or division is responsible to each of its members so that there are specified two-way expectations on the part of both parties.

To achieve these ends the team or division should be a coherent organization that rotates routine tasks on a regular basis, allocates pay fairly in relation to productivity as well as seniority, engages in producing safe and fair working conditions, and defends the rights of its members. Members of each group should hold the group and its managers responsible for their actions, just as the team or group holds its employee-members accountable. Each group should operate like an expanded Scanlon Plan (see Appendix to Chapter 7), embodying awareness of moral rights, autonomy, and human initiative as well as productivity as part of its goals, each member of the team participating as fully as possible in the team's goals. Rewards for each group will be evaluated in terms of initiative and responsibility as well as on the basis of inventive ideas and productivity. The aim of such cooperative efforts is to make each individual an important contributor to the corporate effort. This not only makes work meaningful to employees, but also develops initiative and individual responsibility, all factors that contribute to economic as well as moral well-being.

Part of the reorganization of a corporation should consist in the development of participatory management programs aimed at involving as many persons as possible in the management of the office, plant, or division. Not every person will want to participate, and some will not have the skills to do so, but opportunities should be available for those who want them. And as we saw in Chapter Seven, "flattening the hierarchical structure" by participatory management often contributes to an employee's sense of independence and self-development. It also has proven utilitarian benefits for the organization in terms of employee involvement and increased productivity. To quote a recent survey:

> Excellent companies treat the rank and file as the root source of quality and productivity gain. They do not foster we/they labor attitudes or regard capital investment as the fundamental source of efficiency improvement.[8]

Training programs should be offered to employees to initiate workers into decision-making and management skills and to retool the workplace for technological and product changes. In an evolving work environment employees must be prepared for future employment with proper technological skills. These sorts of programs prepare the employee for changes within the corporation as it responds to new technology and new markets, and enable the corporation to fulfill its implicit job security contract with long-term senior employees without keeping them on after their skills become obsolete. Such training programs are not merely the responsibility of the corporation. Employer encouragement of employee participation in such programs is short-term insurance against long-term disemployment and related employer fiduciary responsibilities, when events such as the recession of the early 1980s occur.

This description has only taken into account group participation in business. To increase loyalty and to recognize fully employees as persons one must strive to make every job a meaningful job for every employee. To accomplish this business must recognize individual differences as well as group responsibilities, as participants in the Bolivar Project learned. Work in any situation should be organized to meet the needs and desires of different personalities. In particular, those doing menial tasks should be given special remuneration or rotated periodically from their assignments, so that they feel like full participants in organizational activities. Those wishing *not* to participate in worker-management teams should be exempt from doing so without co-worker retaliation. And no person should be encouraged to take an assignment or responsibility for which she is unfit. A fair workplace is one that recognizes freedom of choice, individual differences, and human fallibility, as well as the importance of group participation and worker management.

Can this be accomplished in a large bureaucratic corporation? One of the most serious and obvious problems with today's businesses is that constituents often get caught up with roles, positions, rules, and organizational charts rather than with contributions toward the goals of the business.

---

[8]Peters and Waterman, p. 14.

According to a recent analysis, however, successful large corporations can and do "break up" bureaucracy. Operating with a small staff, simplifying the organizational chart, decentralizing responsibility, encouraging a flexible management that can and does change responsibilities frequently, and of course encouraging independent initiative throughout the organization are ways in which many large corporations successfully circumvent the bureaucracy traditionally associated with large organizations.[9]

Corporations are held accountable to their stockholders through representative boards of directors, and they are often held accountable to customers through strict liability legislation, but seldom are they held accountable to their employees. This lack of accountability contributes to a paucity of corporate moral awareness because it allows a corporation to "act" formally, as does Robotron, without having to answer to those it holds accountable: its employees. This lack of accountability encourages employees to perform strongly-differentiated role functions without taking into consideration larger societal issues. Thus employees sometimes act like Robotron's robots. Collective moral awareness is thwarted because constituents, who account for its development, are themselves morally inactive in corporate decision-making. Part of establishing moral awareness and moral activity in corporations, then, is to alter the accountability relationships between corporations and their constituent employees in such a way as to produce a recognized and enforced explicit correlative answerability of the corporation to its employees or to groups or teams of employees. This follows from the essential role of constituent input into corporate "actions," and from the reciprocal nature of employee-employer relationships. Only if corporations are accountable to their constituents, who, after all, make up and determine the character of the organization, will moral relationships between employers and employees be realized and moral input into corporate decision-making processes stimulated.

The accountability of a corporation to its employees is difficult to spell out because we are unused to the concept. The goal of such accountability is to nurture relationships between employees and their corporation such that the corporation, like a nation, becomes answerable to its constituents and can be called to account for not meeting its obligations. This sort of accountability can be achieved only if employees are given prerogatives, similar to stockholder prerogatives, to truly alter those corporate actions to which they justifiably object. This could be accomplished without employee takeover of the corporation. For example, employee committees, as representative segments of the employee corporate population, could have a decisive voice in decision-making policies. Employees could be allowed to evaluate their foremen or managers periodically, a practice that has actually been instituted in a few corporations.

[9]Peters and Waterman, especially pp. 306–17.

One could imagine a series of mutual and correlative accountability relationships within a corporation between employees, groups of employees, divisions, and management something like an organization chart. Unlike a traditional hierarchical organization chart, however, the relationship between each element of the organization would be a two-way reporting relationship such that each person or group of persons on the chart would be not only accountable to, and evaluated by, a second group, but that second group also correlatively answerable to, and judged by, the first, thus establishing moral interaction between every part of the corporation.

On a practical level, persons, groups or institutions often refrain from activities that are going to be made public or evaluated by others. Open reporting in conjunction with reciprocal evaluation of one group within a corporation by another would enable correlative moral relationships to develop. And publicly available written reports are an effective means to evaluate one's own activities and to protect oneself from accusations of wrongdoing. A reward system for ethically valuable contributions coupled with the accountability of each person for his or her business activities would be added incentives for increased moral activity in the workplace.

The two conditions just outlined, the increased role of the individual in the corporation and double-edged accountability schemes should help to establish a corporate-constituent relationship that is a form of partnership. Each partner has different role responsibilities, each may have certain supervisory control over other parties, but each is held answerable to others.

Turning to the relationship between corporate goals, corporate constituents, and the moral activities of corporations, it can be shown that while one cannot change the nature of corporate goal structure without altering the nature of the corporation, one can change the relationship of corporate constituents to those goals in such a way that the goals come to make a moral difference to the constituents. A corporation exists to achieve ends which, in the first instance, are satisfied by the decision-making processes of the organization. These ends are not identified with the well-being of constituents, nor does one expect them to be. Rather, they are the means by which a constituent remains employed, gains economic rewards, or receives dividends. However, without altering this means-ends structure, corporate goals could be articulated to coincide more closely with employee and shareholder interests, intentions and responsibilities, so that the goals of a corporation would make a *moral* difference to its constituents.

The goals of a corporation could be as nearly as possible constituent goals, employees being made, in part, responsible for the selection of goals and for the positive benefits or negative feedback these goals produce. This could be achieved by methods such as those illustrated in our analysis of employee participation in the workplace. For example, groups of employees could be made accountable for the development and/or production of a product. Another way to involve employees directly would be to allocate part of corporate profits to be directly reflected in the salary of each employee. Employees or employee committees could have a say in the goods or services to be offered, in the choice of new product lines, in advertising campaigns, in the use of resources, etc. If a corporation manufactures an item employees or stockholders feel is economically inappropriate or harmful, employees as well as shareholders could have power to initiate the withdrawal of that product from the market. These are only examples of the ways in which the goals of a corporation could be as nearly as possible employee and shareholder goals, and the means-ends structure of the organization could be linked as closely as possible to the interests of its constituents.

Little has been said about the relation of the corporation to a very important constituent, the stockholder who, as owner of the corporation, is an essential component in corporate activity. The reason for this omission is that stockholders have excluded themselves, or have been excluded, from the management of what they own. Thus, most stockholders lack interest in corporate management. As we mentioned in Chapter Three, Milton Friedman has suggested a tax program that would act as an incentive to increase shareholder participation and engage shareholders as active constituents in business. As is well known, Friedman advocates abolishing corporate income taxes. Such taxes amount to double taxation for the shareholder, and they reduce available capital for economic growth. Friedman suggests replacing corporate income taxes with a scheme that would tax shareholders on the total earnings of the corporation rather than only on their dividends. For example, if a corporation earned $100 a share, a holder of ten shares would pay tax on $1000, even if the corporation paid a dividend of only $5 a share, or $500, to the stockholder. By shifting the tax burden solely onto the stockholder, Friedman argues, these persons or institutions would begin to take an active interest in what the corporation does with its earnings. Such a proposal brings ownership involvement back into business, and it is worthy of consideration as a means to increase constituent participation on the shareholder level.[10]

One will wonder why the role of the shareholder should be increased. As an owner, the shareholder receives dividends or suffers losses on account of corporate activities. Shareholder interests in corporate activities are, in theory, represented by the board of directors. But in fact, this is not always the case. Sometimes directors, even outside directors, become so involved in the corporation that they promote the interests of constituents within the corporation at the expense of the stockholder. And sometimes boards do not evaluate in a disinterested way the activities of corporate

[10]Friedman, Chapter 10, especially pp. 172–73.

executives. The shareholder who is not on the board of directors can serve, then, as a check, a moral as well as an economic check, on what happens inside the corporation. Shareholder involvement, then, in addition to being an *obligation* of ownership, is an important element in the development of a morally mature company.

The foregoing is merely an outline for a model of corporate moral agency. Constituents are part of, or own, an organization that functions because of them (although not entirely on their behalf). According to this model, constituent participation in business would become a natural part of corporate operations and corporate moral awareness would increase. As an integrated whole, each part would be correlated to and answerable to every other part so that the corporation and its constituents would be morally answerable for corporate actions. This would not be the end of the corporation or of modern business as we know it. Rather, the idea is to reorganize corporations so that reciprocal accountability relationships between constituents are exercised in which each party is responsible to others, but moral rights and the autonomy of all constituents are equally respected. Such a model permits the corporation to advance its economic aims while honoring constituents' moral rights.

Will corporations adopt this model or a similar framework voluntarily, or will more coercive solutions be necessary? One dare not predict, but the future is not altogether bleak. A recent best-selling book, *In Search of Excellence,* argues that an organization's emphasis on the dignity, respect and importance of every individual in the organization is one of the most important characteristics of corporate excellence as measured by economic as well as by ethical criteria.[11] One hopes that such enthusiasm for the individual is not short-lived but will foster increased corporate interest in its constituents as human as well as productive partners in the business enterprise. If a form of private enterprise is to survive in the climate of increasing pressures for employee rights and corporate moral development, corporate organizational reform is essential. The end of the private enterprise system would mean the end of an economic system that, for all its faults, has provided a decent standard of living for most of a large population. The humanization of that system would enhance its viability as an ethically as well as an economically successful form of life.

[11]Peters and Waterman, Chapter 1.

APPENDIX

A Bill of Rights
For Employees and Employers

EMPLOYEE RIGHTS

1. Every person has an equal right to a job and a right to equal consideration at the job. Employees may not be discriminated against on the basis of religion, sex, ethnic origin, race, color, or economic background.
2. Every person has the right to equal pay for work, where "equal work" is defined by the job description and title.
3. Every employee has rights to his or her job. After a probation period of three to ten years every employee has the right to his or her job. An employee can be dismissed only under the following conditions.
   a. He or she is not performing satisfactorily the job for which he or she was hired.
   b. He or she is involved in criminal activity either within or outside the corporation.
   c. He or she is drunk or takes drugs on the job.
   d. He or she actively disrupts corporate business activity without a valid reason.
   e. He or she becomes physically or mentally incapacitated or reaches mandatory retirement age.
   f. The employer has publicly verifiable economic reasons for dismissing the employee, e.g., transfer of the company, loss of sales, bankruptcy, etc.
   g. Under no circumstances can an employee be dismissed or laid off without the institution of fair due process procedures.
4. Every employee has the right to due process in the workplace. He or she has the right to a peer review, to a hearing, and if necessary, to outside arbitration before being demoted or fired.
5. Every employee has the right to free expression in the workplace. This includes the right to object to corporate acts that he or she finds illegal or immoral without retaliation or penalty. The objection may take the form of free speech, whistle blowing, or conscientious objection. However, any criticism must be documented or proven.

6. The Privacy Act, which protects the privacy and confidentiality of public employees, should be extended to all employees.

7. The polygraph should be outlawed.

8. Employees have the right to engage in outside activities of their choice.

9. Every employee has the right to a safe workplace, including the right to safety information and participation in improving work hazards. Every employee has the right to legal protection that guards against preventable job risks.

10. Every employee has the right to as much information as possible about the corporation, about his or her job, work hazards, possibilities for future employment, and any other information necessary for job enrichment and development.

11. Every employee has the right to participate in the decision-making processes entailed in his or her job, department, or in the corporation as a whole, where appropriate.

12. Every public and private employee has the right to strike when the foregoing demands are not met in the workplace.

EMPLOYER RIGHTS

1A. Any employee found discriminating against another employee or operating in a discriminatory manner against her employer is subject to employer reprimand, demotion, or firing.

2A. Any employee not deserving equal pay because of inefficiency should be shifted to another job.

3A. No employee who functions inefficiently, who drinks or takes drugs on the job, commits felonies or acts in ways that prevent carrying out work duties has a right to a job.

4A. Any employee found guilty under a due process procedure should be reprimanded (e.g., demoted or dismissed), and, if appropriate, brought before the law.

5A. No employer must retain employees who slander the corporation or other corporate constituents.

6A. The privacy of employers is an important as the privacy of employees. By written agreement employees may be required not to disclose confidential corporate information or trade secrets unless not doing so is clearly against the public interest.

7A. Employers may engage in surveillance of employees at work (but only at work) with their foreknowledge and consent.

8A. No employee may engage in activities that literally harm the employer, nor may an employee have a second job whose business competes with the business of the first employer.

9A. Employees shall be expected to carry out job assignments for which they are hired unless these conflict with common moral standards or unless the employee was not fully informed about these assignments or their dangers before accepting employment. Employers themselves should become fully informed about work dangers.

10A. Employers have rights to personal information about employees or prospective employees adequate to make sound hiring and promotion judgments so long as the employer preserves the confidentiality of such information.

11A.   Employers as well as employees have rights. Therefore the right to participation is a correlative obligation on the part of *both* parties to respect mutual rights. Employers, then, have the right to demand efficiency and productivity from their employees in return for the employee right to participation in the workplace.

12A.   Employees who strike for no reason are subject to dismissal.

Any employee or employer who feels he or she has been unduly penalized under a bill of rights may appeal to an outside arbitrator.

Index